Learning Journals and Critical Incidents

Learning Journals and Critical Incidents

Reflective Practice for Health Care Professionals

Second edition

Tony Ghaye and Sue Lillyman

QUAY
BOOKS

A division of MA Healthcare Ltd

Quay Books Division, MA Healthcare Ltd, St Jude's
Church, Dulwich Road, London SE24 0PB

British Library Cataloguing-in-Publication Data
A catalogue record is available for this book

ISBN-13: 978 1 85642 331 1
ISBN-10: 1 85642 331 X

Printed by Ashford Colour Press Ltd, Gosport, Hampshire

To our parents: Marjorie and John, Jean and Reg

Contents

Preface

Reflection and reflective practice are centrally about competence and confidence in clinical practice. All health professionals are required to produce a Personal Development Plan as identified in the Knowledge and Skills Framework (Department of Health, 2004). Practitioners are required to produce evidence of how they have applied learned theory into their practice; here the learning journal and critical incident analysis can assist the practitioner in the production of that evidence.

The knowledge, skills and sensitivities required can be derived from many sources and in different ways. For example, the knowledge can be personal and practical. The skills can be psychomotor, social or cognitive. The sensitivities may be associated with perceptions of dignity, compassion, rights and morality. Additionally, all health care professionals act in context, for example in small or larger teams, within an NHS Trust or community. The context for care is influenced and bounded by people, places and things, all of which are linked and interact in particular ways to try to serve the public interest and common good.

This book is intended to support health care professionals in becoming more personally and publicly accountable. It is therefore educative in its intent in that it tries to help all health care professionals to reflect on what may well be perceived as competent and skilful clinical action. Through the more generic process of reflective practice and the more specific and related approaches of journal writing and critical incident analysis, we hope that health care professionals may be able to make even more sense of their clinical worlds by additionally inquiring into, and understanding more richly, that which is often implicit in everyday practice. In doing so the book takes the reader into a health care landscape which is intellectual, emotional, moral and ethical. Issues of power, policies, interests and truth need to be confronted. We invite you to interact with the text in the spirit of lifelong learning and managing for quality.

Tony Ghaye and Sue Lillyman

Reference

Department of Health (2004) *The NHS Knowledge and Skills Framework and the Development Review Process*. Department of Health, London.

Acknowledgements

In constructing this book we acknowledge our debt of thanks for the support and stimulating dialogues we have had with our colleagues, students and friends who have encouraged us to write a book of this kind.

Introduction

This book is designed to assist health care professionals to develop the art of learning from reflective practice. Journal writing and analysis of critical incidents are two of the ways to facilitate reflection. Specifically they relate to the art of reflection-on-action. This reflection often takes place after an event and out of the critical area.

Reflection is a means of learning from and improving practice (Street, 1991; Johns, 2004), and reflective learning journals are a significant tool in promoting active learning (Thorpe, 2004). Just as the process of health care itself continuously unfurls, so too does reflective practice. Reflection-on-action focuses upon who we are, what we know and what we can do with this to improve the quality of the care we can give.

The book is divided into three broad sections to do with 'context', 'learning processes' and 'outcomes'. In **Part 1: Context**, the genesis, goals and interests of reflective practice are set out. Although the art of reflective practice was formally introduced into the health care arena via the Post-Registration and Practice (PREP) requirements (United Kingdom Central Council, 1992) and the government's *Vision for the Future* (Department of Health, 1993), it is not a new idea and can be traced back to Dewey at the turn of the 20th century. Following on from this we look at the ways in which a variety of writers have organised the processes of learning through reflection into 'models'. A number of models are critiqued and then organised into a typology. Taken together, the two chapters in Part 1 remind us that it is difficult to know what we cannot see. The four chapters in Part 2 give us two lenses to do just this.

Part 2: Process describes and justifies journal writing and critical incident analysis as two ways to learn from reflection-on-action. Examples of each process, drawn from clinical practice, are given. Learning through journal writing and the analysis of critical incidents gives weight to the idea that we should not assume that clinical practice is naturally self-disclosing. It often does not speak for itself. It is not always transparent and familiar. The examples we present and interrogate make the point that the value, significance and meaning of our clinical practice have to be constructed and interpreted. These constructions are historically, politically, economically, socially and culturally determined.

In **Part 3: Outcomes** we take a look at some of the implications for clinical practice that arise from reflecting-on-action through journal writing and critical incident analysis. These processes are appropriate to all health care professionals at any stage of their career. It is through reflection-on-action that individual practitioners and groups of health care professionals generate opportunities to nourish their practice and improve the quality of the care that they provide their client group.

References

Department of Health (1993) *A Vision for the Future. The Nursing, Midwifery and Health Visiting Contribution to Health and Health Care*. Department of Health, London.

Johns, C. (2004) *Becoming a Reflective Practitioner*, 2nd edn. Blackwell, Oxford.

Street, A. (1991) *From Image to Action: Reflection in Nursing Practice*. Deakin University Press, Melbourne.

Thorpe, K. (2004) Reflective Learning Journals: from Concept to Practice. *Reflective Practice*, **5**(3), 327–43.

United Kingdom Central Council (1992) *Post-Registration and Practice*. UKCC, London.

PART I

Context

CHAPTER 1

Reflective practice in perspective

Introduction

In recent years, *reflection* and *reflective practice* have become well-known terms within the health care arena. They are words that have been debated and discussed within the health care setting, nursing, allied health professions, and the medical and social care literature, and have recently become a part of every professional's vocabulary.

This chapter identifies where these terms and concepts originated from and what their place is within clinical practice today. It identifies how they can be used as evidence of personal and professional development. It also demystifies some of the interpretations that writers have given to the area of reflection and reflective practice. These interpretations have caused some confusion and are partially responsible for some of the resistance to the implementation of these concepts in professional practice.

Finally, we discuss how individual practitioners can apply these processes to their clinical practice, identifying how to provide evidence of their professional development in line with their professional bodies' requirements for utilising the skills for their own development.

Historical perspective

Reflection and reflective practice are not new ideas that have recently been identified to complicate the practitioner's life, nor are they unique to the health care arena. Many other professional groups are familiar with the principles and procedures of reflective practice. These include teachers, police officers and other health care professionals.

It was Dewey (1933) who initially defined reflective practice in his work. Over time many others have given their definitions, including Mead (1934), Mezirow (1981), Schon (1987), Burnard (1995), Ghaye *et al.* (1996) and Johns (2004). All the writers on this subject have set out their conceptions in a slightly different way. These multiple interpretations have partially led to the confusion that surrounds the term today.

It is claimed that reflection and reflective practice are an effective means of learning for the individual practitioner (Burnard, 1988; Coutts-Jarman, 1993) as well as a means of maintaining and improving the quality of care given in clinical practice (Burnard, 1991; Clouder and Sellars, 2004). It was through the work of Argyris and Schon (1974) and latterly through Benner (1984) that reflection and reflective practice became fashionable within the education of nurses, midwives and health visitors.

Reflection

There are many definitions in the literature of *reflection*; most, however, agree that it is an active, conscious process (Dewey, 1933; Boud *et al.*, 1985; Schon, 1987; Reid, 1993). Reflection is often initiated when the individual practitioner encounters some problematic aspect of practice and attempts to make sense of it.

Dewey (1933, p. 9) defined reflection as:

> An active persistent and careful consideration of any belief or supposed form of knowledge in the light of the grounds that supports it and the further conclusion to which it tends.

Dewey worked as an educationalist and developed his concept of reflective practice and reflection through *experiential learning* theories. He concluded in his work that the experience the individual lives through can be described as a dynamic continuum and that each experience influences the quality of future experiences.

Boud *et al.* (1985, p. 19) take a different perspective and define reflection as:

> A generic term for those intellectual and effective activities in which individuals engage to explore their experiences in order to lead to a new understanding and appreciation.

Boud and his co-writers view reflection from the learner's point of view. They emphasise the relationship of the reflective process and the learning experience against what the learner can do.

Schon (1987) in his work identifies two types of reflection, these are reflection-*in*-action (thinking on your feet) and reflection-*on*-action (retrospective thinking). He suggests that reflection is used by practitioners when they encounter situations that are unique, and when individuals may not be able to apply known theories or techniques previously learned through formal education. Greenwood (1993), however, identifies weaknesses and inconsistencies in Argyris and Schon's work as they fail to follow their own recommendations. This she argues has resulted in the implementation and prescription of dubious strategies for the promotion of what Schon refers to as enlightened professional artistry. Often formal education cannot answer the complex questions of clinical practice and there remains a gap in knowledge gained. Schon, however. argues that wisdom can be learned by reflection on dilemmas that are encountered in practice and that by using reflection-on-action practitioners can continue to develop their practice.

Reid (1993, p. 305) in her definition also noted reflection as an active process rather than passive thinking. She states:

> Reflection is a process of reviewing an experience of practice in order to describe, analyse, evaluate and so inform learning about practice.

Kemmis (1985) agrees with Reid that the process of reflection is more than a process that focuses 'on the head'. It is, he argues, a positive active process that reviews, analyses and evaluates experiences, draws on theoretical concepts or previous learning and so provides an action plan for future experiences. Johns (1995) notes that reflection enables practitioners to assess, understand and learn through their experiences. It is a personal process that usually results in some change for the individual in their perspective of a situation or creates new learning for the individual.

Reflection starts with the individual or group and their own experiences, and can result, if applied to practice, in improvement of the clinical skills performed by the individual through new knowledge gained on reflection. Clamp (1980) noted that nurses' *attitudes* largely govern how care is administered to their clients, and the commonest causes of poor care are ignorance and inappropriate attitudes. This process of reflection, if then related into practice, can assist the individual in gaining the required knowledge, therefore potentially resulting in an improvement in the *quality of care* received from that individual. The outcome of reflection as identified by Mezirow (1981) is learning.

Louden (1991, p. 149) describes reflection in ordinary language as:

> Serious and sober thought at some distance from action and has connotations similar to 'meditation' and 'introspection'. It is a mental process which takes place out of the stream of action, looking forward or (usually) back to actions that have taken place.

Reflective practice

Once we have decided what reflection is we can then look at reflective practice.

According to Reid (1993, p. 307) reflective practice is:

> Potentially both a way of learning and a mode of survival and development once formal education ceases

Jarvis (1992) refers to reflective practice as 'thoughtful practice': performing actions that are based on known theory and consciously monitoring these actions, questioning why the outcomes occur and thus identifying a widening legitimate knowledge base for the individual. Reflective practice can then not only assist in improving the quality of practice for the individual, but can also assist the individual practitioner in applying formal education and knowledge into clinical practice, thereby applying theory to practice and practice to theory. Reflective practice may also lead practitioners into identifying and justifying their own theories and/or creating a new defensible knowledge. Another aspect of reflective practice is that individuals can justify their practice through reflection on their experiences, being able to identify personal theories, values and beliefs and applying previously learned knowledge to a given situation. Reflective practice, when recorded, can help to assist individuals in recognising and providing evidence of professional and personal development for use in their personal professional profiles.

Learning through experience

Many pre- and post-registration health professionals' courses have included reflective practice as integral components of their programmes. They do not, however, identify how and when the process is to be incorporated.

If we are to use reflection in our experience we will need to re-address the issue of where knowledge comes from and how learning through experience is relevant to the practitioner.

Lewin (1951), in his work relating to social science, identified the complexity of factors that affect learning. He suggests that interaction affects the development of the individual's learning styles, allowing them to know, explain and cope with the experiences they encounter.

Carper (1978) in her work identifies what she refers to as 'Patterns of Knowing'. She suggests four types:

1. Scientific knowledge
2. Personal knowledge
3. Aesthetic knowledge
4. Ethical knowledge

It will be useful to review each of these ways of knowing individually, as reflection and reflective practice will play a major role in gaining and providing evidence of learning through various learning experiences.

Scientific knowledge

This is what Schon (1983) refers to as 'technical rationality' and Burnard (1989) as factual knowledge. This knowledge is gained in health care practice predominantly through formal education, reading and research. It is the science of nursing that can be taught through all courses at both pre- and post-registration levels. Scientific knowledge involves theories that can be learned: they are involved with describing and predicting facts. This scientific knowledge is capable of replication and is therefore given the *scientific* title.

Personal knowledge

This is the knowledge that individuals have acquired through life's experiences. Burnard (1989) refers to it as practice knowledge and Benner (1984) discusses the acquisition of this knowledge through clinical practice. Personal knowledge can be used to identify the difference between what Benner refers to as the advanced beginner and the expert nurse. This knowledge is often not scientifically based and can be generalised.

Aesthetic knowledge

This is what Burnard (1989) refers to as *experiential* knowledge and can be explained as the art of nursing. Benner (1984) refers to the intuition gained through practice that the expert nurse learns through experience. Intuitive judgement is what distinguishes expert human judgement from the decisions or computations that might be made by a beginner or machine (Benner and Tanner, 1987). Aesthetic knowledge is gained through the analysis of the application of theory into practice. It is mainly in this way of knowing that reflection and reflective practice can assist the individual practitioner in coming to terms with experiences and assist them in applying their scientific and personal knowledge into a given situation. The problems encountered with this area are that nursing has traditionally been based upon the scientific medical model. This sits uncomfortably with the idea of aesthetic knowledge. Reflective practice can challenge some of the teaching of health care and can fuel the art versus science debate of nursing practice.

Ethical knowledge

This Benner refers to as the moral knowledge that we all hold and that each of has gained throughout our lives. This knowledge is not to be confused with the legal or ethical knowledge that is learned in formal training. These moral values may at times come into conflict with professional and legal requirements.

Utilising reflection and reflective practice

Reflective practice can be used to identify, justify and assist with the appropriate application of *theory to practice*. This can assist the clinical practitioner in changing care given through a sound knowledge base presented to their client group. It may also provide the practitioner with written evidence of reflection for their personal and professional development in accordance with professional requirements. The written accounts may be used in the classroom to provide a means of applying theory to practice and identifying the application of scientific and personal knowledge in practice. This may also be documented in a personal profile as evidence of learning through practice. The use of documented reflection and reflective practice will be discussed in the following chapters.

Within the Nursing, Health Visitors and Midwives Professional Code of Conduct (Nusing and Midwifery Council, 2002) the need for individual practitioners to be able to justify their practice, and to know their limitations and construct their future action plans, is identified.

The Department of Health (NHSME, 1993) in their paper *A Vision for the Future* identified the need to use reflective skills in their introduction of *clinical supervision*. With the introduction of clinical supervision, reflective practice is essential to identify areas of professional development and can be used as a forum to explore the relation of theory to practice. Gibbs (1988) states that reflection assists in the development of *analytical* skills, moving practitioners away from the descriptive approach and therefore affecting how they perceive their practice. This process may then assist the individual in attaining the competence and supervisory skills required by the *Vision for the Future* recommendations.

Reflective practice can also assist individuals in being able to identify for their own practice the mismatch between the ideology of the profession and the reality of their clinical practice, giving them the ability to adapt and develop their practice in the real world.

Through reflection and reflective practice, individuals utilise the ways of knowing – scientific, personal, ethical and aesthetic knowledge – drawing them together in order to facilitate the development of what Benner (1984) refers to as the 'expert practitioner'.

To conclude, Reid (1993) states that reflective practice is potentially a way of learning and a mode of survival and development for the individual after formal education has finished.

If health care professionals are to gain knowledge across all the areas and to move their practice forward, reflective practice must play an active role in the development of that practice.

The development of reflection assists the individual to gain self-awareness and insight, and provides the ability to express emotion and problem-solving skills, all of which are desirable for professional growth according to Parker *et al.* (1995).

References

Argyris, C. and Schon, D. (1974) Theories of action that inhibit individual learning. *American Psychologist*, **39**, 638–54.

Benner, P. (1984) *From Novice to Expert*. Addison-Wesley, California.

Benner, P. and Tanner, C. (1987) How expert nurses use intuition. *American Journal of Nursing*, **87**(1), 23–31.

Boud, D., Keough, R. and Walker, D. (1985) *Reflection: Turning Experience into Learning*. Kogan Page, London.

Burnard, P. (1988) The journal as an assessment and evaluation tool in nurse education. *Nurse Education Today*, **8**, 105–7.

Burnard, P. (1989) Developing critical ability in nurse education. *Nurse Education Today*, **9**, 271–5.

Burnard, P. (1991) Improving through reflection. *Journal of District Nursing*, **9**(11), 10–12.

Burnard, P. (1995) Nurse educators' perceptions of reflection and reflective practice. *Journal of Advanced Nursing*, **21**, 1167–74.

Carper, B. (1978) Fundamental patterns of knowing. *Advances in Nursing Science*, **1**, 13–23.

Clamp, C. (1980) Learning through critical incidents. *Nursing Times*, 2 October, 1755–8.

Clouder, L. and Sellars, J. (2004) Reflective practice and clinical supervision: an interprofessional perspective. *Journal of Advanced Nursing*, **46**(3), 262–9.

Coutts-Jarman, J. (1993) Using reflection and experience in nurse education. *British Journal of Nursing*, **2**(1), 77–80.

Dewey, J. (1933) *How we Think*. Henrey Regney, Chicago.

Ghaye, A. Cuthbert, S., Danai, K. and Dennis, D. (1996) *Learning through Critical Reflective Practice*. Quayside BDC, Newcastle upon Tyne.

Gibbs, G. (1988) *Learning by Doing: A guide to Teaching Learning Methods.* Oxford Polytechnical, Oxford.

Greenwood, J. (1993) Reflective practice: a critique of the work of Argyris and Schon. *Journal of Advanced Nursing,* **21,** 1044–50.

Jarvis, P. (1992) Reflective practice and nursing. *Nurse Education Today,* **12,** 174–81.

Johns, C. (1995) The value of reflective practice for nursing. *Journal of Clinical Nursing,* **4,** 23–30.

Johns, C. (2004) *Becoming a Reflective Practitioner,* 2nd edn. Blackwell Science, London.

Kemmis, S. (1985) *Action Research and the Politics of Reflection.* Cited in *Reflection: Turning Experience into Learning* (eds. D. Boud, R. Keough and D. Walker). Kogan Page, London.

Lewin, K. (1951) *Field Theory in Social Science.* Harper & Row, New York.

Louden, W. (1991) *Understanding Teaching.* Cassell, London.

Mead, G. (1934) *Mind, Self and Society: From the Standpoint of Social Behaviourist.* University of Chicago Press, Chicago.

Mezirow, J. (1981) A critical theory of adult learning and education. *Adult Education,* **32**(1), 3–24.

NHSME (1993) *A Vision for the Future. The Nursing, Midwifery and Health Visitors Contribution to Health Care.* Department of Health, London.

Nursing and Midwifery Council (2002) *Professional Code of Conduct.* UKCC, London.

Parker, D., Webb, J. and D'Souza, B. (1995) The value of critical incident analysis as an educational tool and its relationship to experiential learning. *Nurse Education Today,* **15,** 111–16.

Reid, B. (1993) 'But we're doing it already!' Exploring a response to the concept of reflective practice in order to improve its facilitation. *Nurse Education Today,* **13,** 305–9.

Schon, D. (1983) *The Reflective Practitioner: How Practitioners Think in Action.* HarperCollins, San Francisco.

Schon, D. (1987) *Educating the Reflective Practitioner.* Jossey Bass, San Francisco.

United Kingdom Central Council (1990) *The Report of Post-Registration Education and Practice Project.* UKCC, London.

CHAPTER 2

A critique of models of reflection

If health care professionals view themselves, or are viewed as, 'technicians', and nursing is seen as embracing Schon's notion of 'technical rationality', there would be little need for books on reflective practice. If, however, health care in general and nurses in particular see themselves as agents of progressive improvements in the quality of care, vision and compassion, the former position collapses and reflective practice becomes a genuinely compelling part of the transformative agenda. This chapter seeks to review a number of different models of reflection. By comparing one with another their similarities and differences will be highlighted. This process will combine a '*discourse of possibility*' (what the models can offer us) with a '*discourse of critique*' (the limitations of the models). This combination seeks to expose the power that models of reflection have to enable health care professionals to become more critically aware of their own values and the extent to which they live these out in their clinical practice, as well as the power they have to transform practice and the clinical context in which it is embedded.

What are models of reflection?

We need to begin with a few broad brush strokes. Models of reflection are characterised by their number and variety. While some are explicitly called 'models of reflection', others are more generally called 'models of learning'. Additionally some require the learner to engage in reflection on practice in a sustained and continuous manner while others include 'reflection' as part of a process which includes other actions or strategies such as gathering data about practice. Some models appear to place greater emphasis on explicating a 'process' of reflection, while others imply that the process is a means to an end, that end being improvements in health care practice. Reflection can also concern itself with the micro aspects of our clinical work – a problematic client, improving a particular aspect of care, changing a routine and so on – to more macro concerns about the culture of a hospital/Trust, ethical principles underlying practice, resource allocations and the like. Whether micro or macro in focus, reflection brings together issues of human agency and structure. In very general terms, though, we could advance that models of reflection, no matter how they are constructed and what they require of us, do share the following qualities:

- They help us to learn from our experience because they are practitioner-focused.
- In doing so they help us to develop a greater sense of personal–professional biography and history.
- They engage us in the process of knowledge creation by helping us to move from tacit knowing to more conscious and explicit knowing.
- They help us to overcome professional inertia by asking us to look at what we do, our taken-for-granted clinical worlds and that which is atypical, 'critical' and professionally significant.
- They intend to add more meaning and ascribe new and relevant meaning to our clinical practice through reflexive conversations with clinical situations. In this sense they enhance meaningful dialogue.
- They have some significance for future personal, and sometimes collective, action.
- They celebrate the role of human agency.

We can summarise the commonalities by suggesting that all models of reflection can be seen from one or more of the following perspectives:

1. **A competency-based perspective**: in that they are to do with clinical skill development, clinical action and improving practice within the contemporary world of the health care delivery system
2. **A personalistic perspective**: in that they are to do with personal agendas, emotionality, self-study and individual enhancement through a greater sense of self-worth and identity

3. **An experiential perspective**: in that nurses are involved in an active exploration of experience that is their experience and that of others. This requires that they value their own experience and have an openness that enables them to lean from the experiences of others (Kolb, 1984).

4. **A transformatory perspective**: in that they are to do with destabilisation because they challenge the status quo, challenge oppressive and disempowering clinical contexts and focus on reducing or removing barriers to improvement

All the models reviewed in this chapter differentially and in particular ways address three overlapping and interacting worlds of the health care professional. They are the:

- **Social world**: for example ward, unit and department cultures or contexts to which reflection refers and in which reflection is located. This social world is made up of feelings, norms, attitudes and values.
- **Behavioural world**: for example of routine and emergency work and the formal and informal rules and protocols which guide and give rise to competent clinical action.
- **Structural world**: for example the overarching internal and external politico-economic and socio-cultural power structures which govern and influence who gets what, where and how and which fundamentally determine the conditions under which health care professionals work.

These three worlds can be linked to Habermas's three generic learning domains (1972) namely the social, the technical and the emancipatory. These domains can be seen as broad ways of modelling reflective practice. The first can be related to personal meanings, to the artistry of generating interpersonal understanding and effective communication. The second is connected to task-related competence and craft knowledge, and to making more efficient that which is already in existence. The third is more radical and has a political agenda in its desire to improve clinical practice through a transformation of current configurations of knowledge, social relations and values that give rise to particular patterns of practice.

One of the first questions that confront us is, 'Which model of reflection should I use?'. Choice is dependent upon criteria. Our choice of model depends upon criteria embedded in each of these two aspects '*of reflection*', to do with conceptualisations and purposes.

Some conceptualisations of reflection are:

- **as a dichotomy** of reflection-in-action and reflection-on-action (Schon, 1983, 1987). The latter is the concern of this text and is a retrospective interrogation of practice to come to know the knowledge used and the feelings that accompanied action within an particular clinical situation. The notion of 'reframing' lies at the heart of this conceptualisation. This is a process where data drawn from our practice is seen differently.
- **as intentional activity** (Ghaye, 1996), in that we reflect on purpose and with a purpose in mind. It is no accident that we reflect. Something usually triggers it.
- **as for knowledge and skill development** (Benner, 1984; Bloom, 1956; Gatley, 1992; Steinmaker and Bell, 1979; Department of Health, 2004), where reflection is claimed to develop and enhance particular cognitive, affective and psycho-motor skills.
- **as creating practitioner-derived knowledge** (Smyth, 1991) which is worthy, valid and relevant to particular clinical situations.
- **as resolving problematic situations** and the basis for problem-based learning (Dewey, 1933; Schon, 1991; Woods, 1994), where systematic reflection enables us to think through and resolve clinical situations which we perceive as being characterised by uncertainty, disorder and indeterminacy.
- **as a process of becoming different** (Giroux, 1987), in which reflection helps us to equip us with the lenses to read the world critically in order to improve it.

Some purposes of reflection are:

- **to act as a bridge** (Silcock, 1994) from tacit knowledge to considered action and from the practice world to the process of theory generation.
- **to enhance the quality of action** (Olsen, 1992; Burrows, 1995) in that it enables us to talk about our clinical practice (critically reflective conversations with self and others) and to practice different things. Reflection without action is just 'wishful thinking' (Freire, 1972).
- **to increase accountability** (Diamond, 1991; Clouder and Sellars, 2004) because the principles of technocratic efficiency emphasise hierarchically structured, 'top down' models of accountability with an increasing burden for professional accountability residing with the individual health carer.
- **as a much needed counter-discourse** (Smyth, 1991) to challenge the esconced and pervasive technicist views of health care practice which marginalise and delegitimate the clinical experiences, histories and practical wisdom nurses use in mediating their lives.

Categories of models of reflection

Our review of the literature on models of reflection has enabled us to categorise them in five ways. All of them aim to 'guide' the reflective process, but do so in different ways. Some are more prescriptive, others give the nurse more freedom to learn. The five models are:

- Structured
- Hierarchical
- Iterative
- Synthetic
- Polycentric

Structured models

In Johns's work (1993, 1994a,b, 2004) he explicitly talks about reflection being a 'profoundly difficult thing to do without expert guidance and support' (Johns, 1994b, p. 110). His intention in constructing a model of guided reflection is to 'enable reflective practitioners to access, make sense of and to subsequently learn through their experiences to become more effective in their practices' (Johns, 1994a, p. 71). At the heart of his structured approach are questions. In fact he describes the model as a series of cues. Figure 2.1 shows how the 'cue questions' fall into five groups and that they are of the 'what', 'why' and 'how' type. The model is structured in the sense that the questions are already prespecified and the health carer works through the set sequence of questions. Johns is insistent that because reflection on practice is often 'tough' and 'frustrating' that it 'should always be supervised or coached in order to support the journey'. (Johns, 1994b)

The central issues which arise from his model are those to do with:

- the linearity of it and the tidy view of learning that this conveys
- the way questions are not owned by the nurse but provided for them

Smyth (1991) has developed another structured model characterised by what he calls 'a number of moments that can be linked to a series of questions' (Smyth, 1991, p. 113) thus (*page 21*):

The following cues are offered to help practitioners access, make sense of and learn through experience.

1   Description
1.1 Write a description of the experience
1.2 What are the key issues within this description that I need to pay attention to?

2   Reflection
2.1 What was I trying to achieve?
2.2 Why did I act as I did?
2.3 What are the consequences of my actions?
     For the patient and family?
     For myself?
     For the people I work with?
2.4 How did I feel about this experience when it was happening?
2.5 How did the patient feel about it?
2.6 How do I know how the patient felt about it?

3   Influencing factors
3.1 What internal factors influenced my decision-making and actions?
3.2 What external factors influenced my decision-making and actions?
3.3 What sources of knowledge influenced, or should have influenced, my decision-making and actions?

4   Alternative strategies
4.1 Could I have dealt better with the situation?
4.2 What other choices did I have?
4.3 What would be the consequences of these other choices?

5   Learning
5.1 How can I make sense of this experience in light of past experience and future practice?
5.2 How do I *now* feel about this experience?
5.3 Have I taken effective action to support myself and others as a result of this experience?
5.4 How has this experience changed my way of knowing in practice?
     ■ Empirics
     ■ Ethics
     ■ Personal
     ■ Aesthetics

Carper, B. (1978) Fundamental patterns of knowing in nursing. *Advances in Nursing Science*, **1**, 13–23.

Figure 2.1 Johns's structured approach. Source: Johns, C. (1994a) Nuances of reflection. *Journal of Clinical Nursing*, **3**, 71–5.

1. DESCRIBE: what do I do?
2. INFORM: what does this description mean?
3. CONFRONT: how did I come to be like this?
4. RECONSTRUCT: how might I do things differently?

The third moment is often the most problematic, for it is here that practice has to be interrogated and questioned. It is where practice is given some legitimacy through a careful analysis of its genesis. As a way of providing more 'structure' to help in this confrontation process Smyth offers a 'series of guiding questions that might include the following' (p. 116)

- What do my practices say about my assumptions, values and beliefs?
- Where did these ideas come from?
- What social practices are expressed in these ideas?
- What is it causes me to maintain my theories?
- What views of power do they embody?
- Whose interests seem to be served by my practices?
- What is it acts to constrain my views of what is possible?

These questions get to the heart of the agency–structure debate. They are phrased in such a way that the forces that serve to liberate or constrain us in our practice are more known and not seen as immutable givens, but are essentially contestable.

Whereas Johns's model is essentially about developing an epistemology of nursing practice, there are parallels between the work of Smyth (1991) and Habermas (1972). Both fuse epistemology with sociology and politics in that together they are concerned with the value-ladenness of practice, the interests that certain practices serve and the structures of power that affect what we do in context. Basing his work on Freudian psychoanalysis and the power of reflection as a way of becoming more emancipated, Habermas proposes a model structured in 'four stages':

Stage 1: A description and interpretation of the existing situation
Stage 2: A penetration of the reasons which brought the existing situation to the form that it takes
Stage 3: An agenda for altering the situation
Stage 4: An evaluation of the achievement of that agenda in practice

Some may argue that understanding a clinical situation better is no guarantee that practice will indeed improve. Similarly, becoming more aware of the impediments to improving practice does not lead us on naturally to improving practice if we are powerless to act to remove these impediments. It may be that the structured approaches of Johns, Smyth and Habermas provide us with an optimistic model. On the other hand, are they overestimating the power of reflection because of their lack of 'guidance' with regard to becoming emancipated?

Hierarchical models

One of the best known models of this kind was developed by Mezirow (1981), where reflection is presented in seven levels with 'reflectivity' at the base of the hierarchy and 'theoretical' at the top. (see Figure 2.2). As soon as reflection is modelled in this way certain assumptions become apparent. The first assumption is that different types or kinds of reflection can indeed be identified and described. The second is that one kind of reflection is more complex than the preceding one. Thirdly, this complex-

---

1. **Reflectivity**
   The act of becoming aware of a specific perception, meaning or behaviour of your own or the habits you have of seeing, thinking and acting.
2. **Affective**
   Becoming aware of how you feel about the way you are perceiving, thinking or acting.
3. **Discriminant**
   Assessing the efficacy of your perceptions, thoughts and actions. Recognising the reality of the contexts in which you work and identifying your relationship to the situation.
4. **Judgemental**
   Making and becoming aware of your value judgements, about your perceptions, thoughts and actions, in terms of being positive or negative.
5. **Conceptual**
   Being conscious of your awareness and being critical of it (e.g. being critical of the concepts you use to evaluate a situation).
6. **Psychic**
   Recognising in yourself the habit of making precipitant judgements about people based on limited information
7. **Theoretical**
   Becoming aware of the influence of underlying assumptions upon your judgement.

Figure 2.2 Mezirow's seven levels of reflection (Mezirow, 1981).

ity is empirically verifiable. Fourthly, the benefits from reflection accrue by climbing the 'ladder' or ascending the hierarchy. Fifthly, 'mastery' at one level is a prerequisite for moving onto the next level. Finally, learning develops by some process of inclusion, in that later levels encapsulate all that which has gone before.

Models of this kind are a variant of a structured model with the underlying structural variable being based upon the notion of increasing complexity. Van Manen (1977) and Goodman (1984) have provided similar hierarchical models based upon three levels of reflection, namely:

- Practices needed to reach given objectives
- Reflection of the links between principles and practice
- Reflection which incorporates the above and ethical and political concerns.

Iterative models

These models are principally based upon the idea that the reflective process is most appropriately described as a 'cycle' and that deepening awareness and increases in knowledge and skilfulness arise from repeated 'clockwise' movements around the reflective cycle. Gibbs (1988) provides a general cyclical model having six stopping points, with each point on the cycle being associated with a key question (Figure 2.3). In iterative models

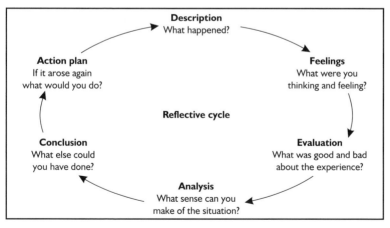

Figure 2.3 Reflective cycle (Gibbs, 1988).

the ongoing nature of learning begins to be signalled. Unlike the previous two model types, reflective cycles have an 'unfinished business' feel to them. Out of the 'Action plan' stopping point come new clinical actions, encounters and situations that can be understood by again asking the question 'What happened?'.

Atkins and Murphy (1994) draw upon the work of others to develop their own cyclical model (Figure 2.4). Although they state that it is possible to begin the reflective process by reflecting on achievements, their model is drawn so that it explicitly shows the process starting with an 'awareness of uncomfortable feelings and thoughts'. To the inexperienced eye their cyclical model conveys the message that reflection always starts with something 'negative', 'uncertain' and 'unsatisfactory'. Its strength, like that of Gibbs (1988), lies in the fact that it endeavours to incorporate knowledge, feelings and action in one learning cycle.

There are two main variants of the iterative model. The first, by Boud *et al.* (1985) captures, among other things, more of the messiness of learning through reflection (Figure 2.5). Their model cleverly holds one cycle of three parts, together with two movements. First there is a cycle which

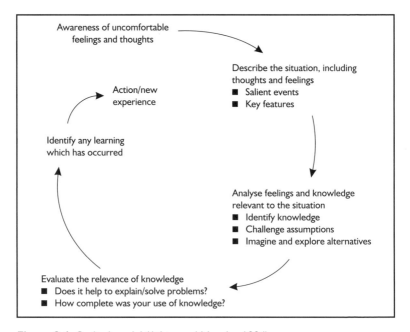

Figure 2.4 Cyclical model (Atkins and Murphy, 1994).

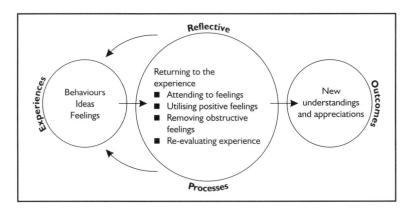

Figure 2.5 Iterative model (Boud *et al.*, 1985).

essentially moves anticlockwise. Here the learner revisits earlier experiences. Then there is another cycle which moves clockwise and connotes that reflection is not just a retrospective process but also a prospective one. The central cycle is characterised by the processes of deconstruction and reconstruction. The second variant is captured in the action research literature (Ghaye *et al.*, 1996a) (Figure 2.6). This is worth mentioning for

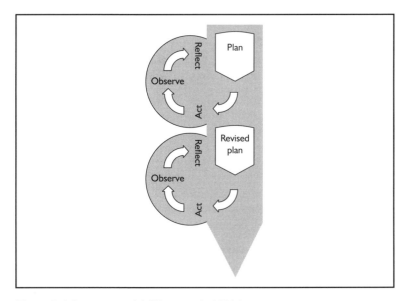

Figure 2.6 Iterative model (Ghaye *et al.*, 1996a).

three reasons. First, the notion of a cycle of learning is complexified and presented as a 'learning spiral'.

The second reason is that reflection is just one 'moment' in the spiral process. The moments are:

- Plan
- Act
- Observe
- Reflect
- Replan

The third reason is that the spiral conveys a clear message that having gone through these moments we never return to the same place and start again. The planning, acting, observing and reflecting at least move our thinking forward, if not our clinical practice or the context in which it is located. The problem is that we need to be able to validate any claims that we make that we have indeed moved on.

Synthetic models

In an excellent text by Louden (1991) we find a very useful synthetic model of reflection. By synthetic we mean that in attempting, 'to clear a conceptual path through the variety of ways in which the term reflection has been employed' (Louden, 1991, p. 149) he has brought together in one holistic model two of the critical aspects of reflection, namely:

- the *interests* of reflection: these are the goals or ends of the act of reflection
- the *forms* of reflection: these are the characteristics of the act of reflection

In Figure 2.7 we see that this synthetic model builds on Habermas's (1972) framework and is portrayed as a four-by-four matrix. The two dimensions of the matrix, he argues, are both different and complementary. What is important to grasp is that each act of reflection has both an interest and a form. Louden identifies four types of 'interest':

- **Technical**: an interest in standards, competencies and the development of technical skills.
- **Personal**: an interest in personal meaning and understanding and how this shapes how we feel and act.

- **Problematic**: an interest in the resolution of problems of clinical action
- **Critical**: an interest in questioning taken-for-granted thoughts, feelings and actions.

	Forms			
Interests	Introspection	Replay and rehearsal	Enquiry	Spontaneity
Technical				
Personal				
Problematic				
Critical				

Figure 2.7 Synthetic model (Louden, 1991).

The four 'forms' of reflection are:

- **Introspection**: is similar to Schon's reflection-on-action reflection in that it is deliberate contemplation of a past event at some distance from the stream of action.
- **Replay and rehearsal**: where events are reworked in our heads and gone over again, and might also involve the nurse talking about an event that has happened or which might happen in the future.
- **Enquiry**: where there is a deliberate and explicit connection between thinking and doing. This lies close to a tenet of action research in that it is a planned intervention, a deliberate move to systematically look into something.
- **Spontaneity**: where reflection is so bound up in the moment of the action that there is no conscious awareness of thinking about the action. It is tacit reflection which takes place within the stream of experience. It is what Schon would call reflection-in-action.

One of the strengths of this model is that it helps us to appreciate what other models do and can offer us. For example we can now re-view the previous three model types and interrogate them with questions of the kind, 'Do they connect a single interest with a single form?', 'Do they connect a single interest with a range of forms?' and so on. This model also acts as a catalyst in that it invites us to think about how separate and exhaustive the boxes and categories are. Finally, the synthetic model allows us to appreciate some of the subtleties of learning from experience, as in the course of one conversation with a mentor, clinical supervisor or preceptor, a practitioner may move from a focus on one form and interest to another.

Holistic models

As with synthetic models, holistic models which are flexible and explicitly value-based have yet to become established in the reflective development of health care professionals. Figure 2.8 is an example of a holistic model. Here Ghaye (1996) argues that a model of reflective practice should align itself with a complex and dynamic health care system and a rapidly changing health care environment. In a range of texts, Ghaye *et al.* (1996b) set out what they call their model of the 'practitioner-as-learner', where reflection facilitates improvements in the quality of an individual's work and link this closely with improvements in practice areas themselves. The model is an 'opportunity to learn' and is premised upon the idea that learning is enhanced through critical reflection and that critical reflective practice does make a difference. Their polycentric model embraces eight learning principles:

- The model is enabling rather than prescriptive.
- Reflection should begin with a consideration of individual and collective professional values and what it means to be a professional and that after this the learner is free to engage in any other reflective cycle as long as the choice is a conscious and justifiable one.
- Improving practice requires the health care professional to see holistically and think in a multidisciplinary way.
- Improving practice requires a high level of skill in being able to transfer, apply and modify knowledge from other fields.
- Just as work conditions change so do the concepts and categories that we use to make sense of our professional practice. This requires the

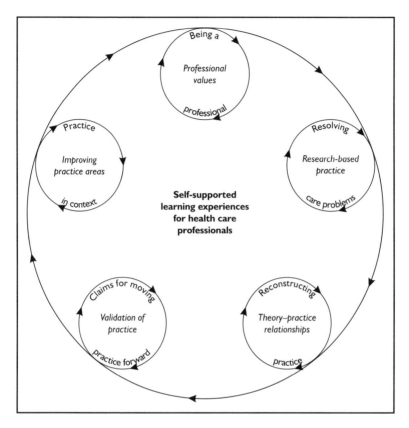

Figure 2.8 Holistic model (Ghaye, 1996b).

nurses to interrogate the ways in which they habitually make sense of their practice.

- Reflective and reflexive practice must interact if meaningful, relevant and sustainable improvement is to take place.
- Improving practice requires us to reflect upon the very nature or essence of our professionalism.
- Practice can be improved and learning facilitated through the establishment and nourishment of a community of reflective health care professionals engaging in peer group dialogue.

For Ghaye (1996), critically reflective practice involves questioning:

- accepted understanding about health care practice;

- received 'truths' about the nature and power of individual and collective competence;
- the relevance and generation of 'know-that', 'know-how' and 'know-why' knowledge.

Reflection is a complex business. This holistic model reflects this complexity and gives the health carer the freedom to learn within an enabling framework. It places the responsibility for learning on the shoulders of the individual or group of learners and also explicitly addresses the ethical dimension of reflecting on practice. Individuals are encouraged to monitor improvements in their thinking and clinical practice by periodically checking where they 'feel they are at' on a 5 × 5 matrix (Table 2.1) The vertical axis shows five different types of 'reflection-on-practice'. The horizontal axis shows five reflective cycles which together comprise this holistic model. They are cycles which focus learning on:

- 'My professional values'
- 'Researching my practice and resolving care problems'
- 'Looking at my practice in relation to the work of others'
- 'Setting out and supporting a claim that my practice has moved forward'
- 'Trying to improve my practice area'

In judging the worthwhileness and usefulness of each of these models the following should be borne in mind. Some models of reflection appear to be value-neutral or value-blind in that they do not talk about professional values. Some models focus on practice deficits and tend to convey a message that they need only to be used when something goes wrong. Some models present learning through reflection as a tidy, one-way and unproblematic process. What are the strictures in the structures, hiccups in the hierarchies and calamities in the cycles? Some appear to be trapped in a psychologistic framework ignoring health care as a moral and ethical art form, while others focus only on the private, individual and particular clinical world, not the wider public world of social and political action. Some emphasise self-understanding which may not be a basis for altering the existing structures and arrangements. Some emphasise personal deliberation and contemplation rather than active, militant confrontations with practice infused with understandings of power and politics. Finally, some models of reflection place a greater emphasis on self-empowerment, while others are more focused on critique and possibility. Above all else, each model has strengths and limitations.

In some ways each of these five types of model of reflection can claim that they have the potential to:

- Foster the development of a more emancipated, enlightened and empowered health care professional
- Develop certain individual virtues like justice, honesty and courage
- Cast the health carer in the active role of meaning-maker
- Resolve contradictions and conflicts in clinical practice
- Link issues of agency with structure

However, the continued use of models of reflection will only occur if we are able to present valid claims that learning through reflection improves the quality of client care. Much more research needs to be done to support such a claim.

References

Atkins, S. and Murphy, K. (1994) Reflective practice. *Nursing Standard*, **8**(39), 49–56.

Benner, P. (1984) *From Novice to Expert*. Addison-Wesley, New York.

Bloom, B. (1956) *A Taxonomy of Educational Objectives*. McKay, New York.

Boud, D. *et al.* (1985) Promoting reflection in learning: a model. In *Reflection: Turning Experience into Learning* (eds. D. Boud, R. Keough and D. Walker). Kogan Page, London.

Burrows, D. (1995) The nurse teacher's role in the promotion of reflective practice. *Nurse Education Today*, **15**, 346–50.

Clouder, L. and Sellars, J. (2004) Reflective practice and clinical supervision: an inter-professional perspective. *Journal of Advanced Nursing*, **46**(3), 262–9.

Dewey, J. (1933) *How We Think: a Restatement of the Relation of Reflective Thinking to the Educative Process*. Heath & Co., New York.

Diamond, P. (1991) *Teacher Education as Transformation*. Open University Press, Milton Keynes.

Department of Health (2004) *The NHS Knowledge and Skills Framework (NHS KSF) and the Development Review Process*. Department of Health, London.

Freire, P. (1972) *Pedagogy of the Oppressed*. Penguin, Harmondsworth.

Gatley, E. (1992) PREPP: From novice to expert. *British Journal of Nursing*, **1**(2), 88–91.

Ghaye, T. (1996) *An Introduction to Learning Through Critical Reflective Practice*. Formword Publications, Newcastle-upon-Tyne.

Ghaye, T. *et al.* (1996a) *Research-based Practice: Resolving Care Problems*. Formword Publications, Newcastle-upon-Tyne.

Ghaye, T. *et al.* (1996b) *Learning through Critical Reflective Practice: Self-Supported Learning Experiences for Health Care Professionals*. Pentaxion Press, Newcastle-upon-Tyne.

Table 2.1 Holistic model: reflection matrix (Ghaye et al., 1996b).

Types of reflection	Cycle 1 *Professional values: being a professional*	Cycle 2 *Research-based practice: resolving care problems*	Cycle 3 *Theory–practice relationships: reconstructing practice*	Cycle 4 *Validation of practice: claims for moving practice forward*	Cycle 5 *Improving practice areas: practice in context*
Critical	Able to evaluate the link between own professional development and organisational improvement. Can question organisational practice and policy constructively but critically, to reveal contradictions between organisational rhetoric and realities. Can construct rationale for transforming organisational culture to make it more emancipatory and empowering.	Reflect fully upon the moral and ethical implications of research-based practice. Draws upon research to enlighten, empower and challenge their own and others' practice. Uses research to point to individual and collective contradictions in practice. Reflects upon the way research can constructively challenge the status quo.	Sees theory as able to question clinical habits, traditions and prevailing ideologies. Uses theory to enlighten their practice and emancipate it from the causal influences and structures that constrain it. Clearly able to 'theorise' about those things that constrain or liberate their practice.	Able to evaluate personal and collective claims for moving practice forward by linking them to notions of enlightenment, emancipation and empowerment. Can critique claims by adopting a position of reflective scepticism and by using both dialogical and dialectical thinking.	Able to synthesise individual and collective improvements with systemic and cultural improvements in the organisation. Can evaluate links between enhanced professionalism, improvements in practice, and more empowered health carers. Can conceptualise and critique workplace improvement as a democratic struggle about rights, fairness, justice and improved care.
Interactive	Able to link contradictions in practice to action plans for individual and collective improvement. Thorough understanding of internal/external influences that impact on own professional values and practice area values. Can articulate political and ethical consequences of action plans to improve thinking and practice.	Able to articulate the reasons why research-based practice is important. Through reflection, can link research with improvements in health care in their own practice area. Able to plan, implement and evaluate collaborative practice-based research. Opens up research so that others may critique it. Appreciates how value-laden the research process is. Uses the outcomes of research to reflect upon the nature of the relationship between practice and theory.	Able to articulate an interactive view of the relationship between theory and practice. Can justify a position that practice is theory-laden. Able to generate and defend their own practical theory.	Can set up validation events. Able to link the construction of a claim with the process of validating claims by self and through a peer group validation event. Can act in the role of critical friend. Can initiate, sustain and evaluate the critical dialogues that arise through the validation process.	Able to articulate links between desired improvements in the quality of action and improvements in client care. The impact of the improvement effort on all concerned can be justified. Thorough understanding of the influences on 'total quality'. Able to develop, implement and evaluate action plans to improve practice area culture.

Table 2.1 (continued)

Receptive	Can publicly justify practice with reference to personal and organisational values. Can identify self as a living contradiction and present evidence to illuminate this. Able to position personal values in relation to personal history, others' practice and the professional literature. Able to critique own espoused values and values-in-action.	Can justify what to research and how to do it. Through reflection, can identify and explain the problem, issue, concern or question they wish to research. Able to position their 'new' knowledge relative to other relevant research. Appreciates the importance of research being systematic, rigorous and valid.	Is able to justify where their own health care knowledge comes from. Can make sound connections between 'know how to', and 'know why' knowledge. Able to make judgements about the knowledge they and others should possess. Does not 'position' theory as opposite to practice, but integrated with practice. Able to articulate and explain links between 'what they say', and 'what they do'.	Able to publicly justify, in a clearly understandable manner, a claim that personal thinking and/or practice has moved forward. Able to distinguish between particular and general claims. Can position own claim in relation to other claims found in the professional literature. Able to make a reasoned judgement about the validity of others' claims.	Can publicly justify improvements to personal practice. Distinguishes between change and improvement and can present evidence to illuminate this. Sees improvement as a complex political and moral enterprise. Able to position personal improvement efforts in relation to literature on organisational development and training.
Perceptive	Developing consciousness of the significance and nature of professional values that give practice a shape, form and purpose. Can link descriptions of practice with explanations of practice, but not tie these into personal value positions. Personal practice events explained in relation to past practice and personal feelings towards practice.	Feels that research is intimidating, rather abstract, and often does not help them to resolve 'everyday' practice-based problems. Feels that it is the responsibility of others to generate/extend the knowledge base of the profession. Feels poorly equipped to undertake 'serious' research. Feels under pressure to make their practice more accountable and evidence-based. Feels research is for others, while practice is for them.	Enjoys the world of practice and is intimidated by theory. Feels that theory is abstract and practice is more concrete. Feels under pressure to use theory to justify their practice. Believes that a gap between theory and practice is right and natural. Feels that theory is acquired out of the workplace and has to be 'fitted' to practice. Does not feel equipped to defend a view that their practice is theory-laden.	Knows which areas of practice they feel (un)comfortable with, and can explain this. Aware of the significance and value-ladenness of the phrases 'making a claim' and 'validating practice'. Can express personal feelings about moving practice forward and the effects of routine, busyness, availability of professional development opportunities, family commitments etc on their practice.	Can articulate those aspects of personal practice which provoke anxiety, joy and so on. Can explain improvements with reference to personal experience. Knows that some get hurt in the improvement process. Improvement seen principally as a social business involving people and their feelings. Also improvement as 'doing the right thing', thus involving values, choices and dilemmas.
Descriptive	Tacit awareness of practice guided by professional values. Can describe practice – the 'what' and 'how' – accurately and comprehensively. Can contextualise practice. Able to present a vivid portrayal of self as a professional.	Can describe health care problems and can give a personal view about their resolution. Does not research their own practice. Mainly reads research papers when attending continuing education courses. Often caricatures research as 'grand', 'high status', 'involving large samples' and 'hypotheses'. Thinks research is something done by others. Has a tacit awareness of the importance of research for enhancing good practice.	Can give a personally meaningful definition of the term 'practical knowledge' and can relate this to concrete examples drawn from clinical practice. Describes practice mainly in terms of common-sense ways of knowing. Sees knowledge as outsider knowledge which is applied to practice. Can describe how knowledge has been acquired in training. Separates practice and theory.	Can describe what is known and how worthy they claim this knowledge is. Has a tacit awareness of the multiple meanings of 'practice', and the different ways that knowledge of and for practice is generated. Able to describe own practice and identify areas where practice has moved forward over time. Descriptions tied closely with professional biography and clinical interests.	Awareness that improvements in personal practice can be made. Tacit acknowledgement of the complexity of the improvement process. Can describe personally desirable improvements and contextualise them. Improvement seen principally as doing it right, as more of the same, just better. Improvement is seen mainly as a technical business.

Gibbs, G. (1988) *Learning by Doing: A Guide to Teaching and Learning Methods.* Further Education Unit, Oxford Brookes University, Oxford.

Giroux, H. (1987) Educational reform and the politics of teacher empowerment. *New Education*, **9**(1–2), 3–13.

Goodman, J. (1984) Reflection in teacher education: a case study and theoretical analysis. *Interchange*, **15**(3), 9–26.

Habermas, J. (1972) *Knowledge and Human Interests*. Heinemann, London.

Johns, C. (1993) Professional supervision. *Journal of Nursing Management*, **1**, 9–18.

Johns, C. (1994a) Nuances of reflection. *Journal of Clinical Nursing*, **3**, 71–5.

Johns, C. (1994b) Guided reflection. In *Reflective Practice in Nursing: The Growth of the Professional Practitioner* (eds. A. Palmer, S. Burns, and C. Bulman). Blackwell Scientific Publications, Oxford.

Johns, C. (2004) *Becoming a Reflective Practitioner*, 2nd edn. Blackwell Science, London.

Kolb, D. (1984) *Experiential Learning: Experience as the Source of Learning and Development*. Prentice Hall, New Jersey.

Louden, W. (1991) *Understanding Teaching*. Cassell, London.

Mezirow, J. (1981) A critical theory of adult learning and education. *Adult Education*, **32**(1), 3–24.

Olsen, J. (1992) *Understanding Teaching*. Open University Press, Milton Keynes.

Schon, D. (1983) *The Reflective Practitioner: How Professionals Think in Action.* Temple Smith, London.

Schon, D. (1987) *Educating the Reflective Practitioner*. Jossey Bass, San Francisco.

Schon, D. (ed.) (1991) *The Reflective Turn: Case Studies in and on Educational Practice*. Teachers College Press, New York.

Silcock, P. (1994) The process of reflective teaching. *British Journal of Educational Studies*, **42**(3), 273–85.

Smyth, J. (1991) *Teachers as Collaborative Learners*. Open University Press, Milton Keynes.

Steinmaker, N. and Bell, N. (1979) *The Experiential Taxonomy – A New Approach to Teaching and Learning*. Academic Press, London.

Van Manen, M. (1977) Linking ways of knowing with ways of being practical. *Curriculum Enquiry*, **6**(3), 205–28.

Woods, D. (1994) *Problem-Based Learning: How to Gain the Most from PBL*. McMaster University Press, Hamilton, Ontario.

PART 2

Processes

CHAPTER 3

Enhancing learning through journal writing

The term 'journal' often means different things to different people, with no consensus regarding how to define it (Holly, 1987, 1989; Ballantyne and Packer, 1995; Thorpe 2004). It is more commonly associated with references to 'diaries', 'learning logs' and 'experiential workbooks'. It is dangerous to use these terms synonymously, for there are shades of difference between them. Although they can all claim to enhance learning, each one can also claim to place a different emphasis on the role of self and others in the learning process, on how private or public the document is, on the formality or informality of it, the structure of each entry, how learning emerges and who might benefit. This chapter sets out our conception of a learning journal for health care professionals. The discussion focuses upon responses to a series of questions we are most frequently asked about learning through journal writing.

Why should I keep a professional learning journal?

There are political, professional and personal reasons for keeping a learning journal. Politically there is much being written about improvements in the health of the nation (Department of Health, 1989a,b, 1993, 2004). Embedded in these policy statements are rallying cries for each registered practitioner to be personally accountable for their practice. Keeping a learning journal is a way of developing the skills to become more accountable. The journal can be a repository for professional experiences which can be interrogated, deconstructed and re-evaluated to deepen awareness, enrich skillfulness and enable the health carer to construct robust justifications for their practice and valid arguments for improving their practice areas.

There are three very important professional reasons for keeping a learning journal. The first is the belief that journal writing is a *necessary skill for lifelong learning*. There is an emphasis within the health care arena to education as a lifelong learning process (English National Board, 1991, 1994; Department of Health, 2004). Enmeshed in this discourse are descriptions of lifelong learners as 'change agents' and 'creative' practitioners who are 'responsible and accountable' for their work. The learning that can arise from keeping a journal has the potential to develop these qualities. The notion of a learning journal is now firmly embedded in the practice of health care professionals' education. In essence it helps health carers to develop the ability to be realistic judges of their own performance and, through the writing process, monitor what they claim to know and what remains to be known and practised.

The second reason is that journal writing is *necessary for effective clinical learning*. Effective learning (Boud, 1996, pp. 14–15):

> ... involves learners being able to influence their own learning rather than waiting for others to do so, that is, being proactive. Those who are dependent on the continued impetus of teachers or workplace supervisors to develop and assess their knowledge and skills are severely handicapped in their learning.

This second reason has huge implications for individual health carers, those responsible for the management of pre- and post-registration courses, and those involved in clinical supervision, mentoring and preceptorship. It raises issues about promoting and acquiring learning-how-to-learn skills, about autonomy and self-direction, about responsibilities for learning, and about the role of critical reflection in the interrogation and reconstruction of practice.

The third reason is that journal writing has the potential to *add value to pre- and post-registration courses*. The added value arises principally from the way the journal helps practitioners to focus attention on the impact that the course has on them. In this way the journal has something important to contribute to the professionalisation of the health carer: the development of status and confidence. It adds value because it can act as a bridge between the knowledge, skills and sensitivities that practitioners are acquiring on the one hand, and their application and impact in the clinical environment on the other.

There are a host of personal reasons why it is currently opportune to keep a learning journal. If enhancing practice is about personal improvement linked to organisational development and meaningful, conscious action, then the art of critical reflection becomes a prerequisite. Reflection touches a need within professionals to make sense of their situation. Keeping a learning journal is a way in which tacit knowledge can be set out for inspection and interrogation. It is a way of turning experience into learning.

Learning through journal writing illustrates our understanding of both the nature and generation of health care knowledge. In promoting learning journals we are advocating the view that reality is a social construction (Berger and Luckmann, 1976; Guba and Lincoln, 1989). By this we are suggesting three things. Firstly, to act in a responsible, ethical and competent manner we need to understand and practice with good intentions in our clinical worlds. To do this we need to be aware that each of us, regardless of whether we work in the same area of clinical specialism, apprehends the world differently. So reality is not a fixed and universally agreed objective reality. Reality differs from individual to individual and arises because of our differing expectations, experience, intentions, values and so on. Secondly, we believe that we all exist in a social world. Our clinical action occurs in social spaces which are a web of human relationships comprised of such things as traditions, norms, roles, protocols, power relationships, class and gendered space. Thirdly, competent practice suggests that we try to apprehend the reality of our everyday clinical worlds as an ordered reality. In doing so we build or construct a world which has personal meaning and in which we can act competently and responsibly. Reality is not simply 'there', neutral and self-evident to all, but has to be apprehended and personally constructed. The process of journal writing is one of reality construction.

Our practice often occurs in a turbulent, changing and chaotic environment, in organisations where oppressive politico-social structures often constrain our working lives. Critical reflective practice, enhanced through journal writing, and with its prime concerns of a more enlightened, emancipated and empowered professional, helps us to recognise the structures that constrain and those which enable and facilitate. Through journal writing we can come to know what can be influenced and improved and in what ways.

The learning journal can be 'positioned' in the growing field of narrative research and is a way of understanding how individuals and groups of health care professionals experience and live out their professional lives. The learning journal helps us to define and redefine our purposes, to locate and reconstruct our values and to fix our affective orientation to people and things within our organisation. In this sense the learning journal is concerned with developing an epistemology of health care practice. It focuses on learning from experience and on making sense of the practical events in our professional lives. It enables us not only to describe and explain our practice, but also to justify it. Knowledge generated through keeping a journal is also about the problematic areas of truth-seeking, about professionals as researchers in their own clinical context, and about action as a technical and moral enterprise.

What do I put into a learning journal?

A learning journal should contain practical knowledge (Ghaye *et al.*, 1996a) and wisdom and needs to be understood in content and process terms. *What* is written about, the phenomenon in other words, is the content. When written down, a 'text' is created which enables the nurse to re-examine fundamental issues associated with their professional identity and the contexts which mould it. The text can utilise historical, emotional, personal and clinical data in a creative and interpretative manner so that the meanings that reveal themselves from the re-examination of journal entries at a later date can inform current and future clinical practice.

How the phenomenon is written about, the media and genres used, is the writing process. Learning accrues from this process and is facilitated by responses to questions such as, 'What kind of health care professional am I?', 'How have I come to practice in this way?' and 'How can I improve my practice?'. McNiff (1990, p. 56) reflects on how writing can help to make learning happen:

> In writing I tap my tacit knowledge.... My writing becomes both symbolic expression of thought (this is what I mean) and the critical reflection on that thought (do I really mean this?) My writing is both reflection on action (what I have written) and reflection in action (what I am writing). The very act of making external, through the process of writing, what is internal, ... allows me to formulate explicit theories about the practices I engage in intuitively.

Health care professionals know their practical worlds in general, social and shared ways and also in unique and personal ways. In constructing accounts of practice the past is not irrelevant but provides a context for present thinking and action and future intentions. The practical knowledge that characterises the content of a learning journal reaffirms the view that health carers hold and actively use knowledge of this kind to guide their clinical action and shape their practice area. Entries in the learning journal, if done systematically over time, provide an opportunity to appreciate more richly that this practical knowledge is something which is dynamic and held in an active relationship with practice, and is something which gives it its shape, form and purpose.

You can write about 'critical learning incidents'. These are events or situations which are professionally significant to you. They may, on further reflection, mark a significant change or turning point in your learning. They may cause you to stop and think about what you believe in, say and do (see Chapter 6). You can write about your 'educational/professional values'. Values make you the kind of professional that you are. (Ghaye *et al.*, 1996b). They provide a rationale for what you do. You can write about how far you are able to live out your values in your work, and what helps and hinders this. You can write about the contradictions.

Learning journals serve many purposes, which in turn condition what you write in them. For example, they can serve as a data collection tool for examining changes in your self-image, as an evaluation mechanism for aspects of your practice, to facilitate critical thinking, to release feelings and frustrations, to see different 'truths' and to develop observational skills. Above all else, the learning journal should contain that which is most relevant and meaningful to you, and should do so in a form that you find most liberating. You do not have to write an essay for every entry! You can use jottings, annotated drawings with some writing underneath, concept maps, and so on. You need to set out your entry in sufficient detail that enables you to hook back into it and understand things, as they were, at a later date. You might write in a file or a notebook. It is often useful to work out how you could add new thoughts and perspectives to earlier entries. For example, you might write on the opposite side or reverse side of the paper in your file, or add new pages to it to make it an ever expanding learning journal! It is important to give each entry a date and time.

In the work of Thomas (1992) we can find a number of issues and arguments which can be applied to the nature and educative potency of learning through journal writing. We have drawn upon his work and our own to develop a number of 'portraits' of 'The Clinical/Professional Learning Journal'.

Portrait 1: The learning journal as: 'A collection of anecdotes'

Personal anecdotes are experiences and so have a value. A collection of anecdotal evidence may reveal something worthwhile about clinical thinking, feelings and practice. To be more useful the anecdotes need to be placed in a context and need to be re-visited, re-read and evaluated over time. If anecdotes tell you nothing about how to improve what you do, then you need to change the content and process.

Portrait 2: The learning journal as: 'An interpreted story'

Just as stories have structures, entries in a journal can be structured also. An entry must have a clear beginning and a middle. It might not have an end, just more 'chapters'. As with story-making, the content needs to be carefully selected and certain aspects of the entry given more emphasis than others. Storying also implies telling and listening, which in turn relates to the ethical issue of consent (see below). Finally, journal entries of this kind, just like stories, have to be interpreted. Out of this comes the learning.

Portrait 3: The learning journal as: 'A fulcrum for professional development'

Some of the characteristics of learning-enriched clinical environments are collegiality, open communication, trust, support and help. Having the time to talk through the problems of practice is also a vital ingredient of both personal and collective professional development. For some, the learning journal fulfils a need to tell, to enter into dialogues and to expose and explore various interpretations of 'This is what I did, for these reasons, this is what it felt like, so what do you think?'.

Portrait 4: The learning journal as: 'A means of asserting that your practice is evidence-based'

This can be done if entries are guided by the following: (a) that you are trying to live out the things you believe in; (b) that you wish to account for your actions; (c) that you are actively seeking to improve your practice; and (d) that you acknowledge that claims for moving practice forward have to be supported by evidence.

Portrait 5: The learning journal as: 'A means of bringing order to turbulent clinical environments'

Practice areas have been described as being busy, dis/empowering, un/predictable, confusing, stressful, routine and unique. In trying to make sense of our practice worlds we need to hold the turbulence still for a moment. A single journal entry is a piece of frozen text waiting to be reflected upon. For a moment it brings a kind of order to things. Health care professionals are not confronted with issues, challenges, dilemmas and problems that are independent of each other, but with dynamic, turbulent and often chaotic situations which interact simultaneously. Ackoff (1979) calls such situations 'messes'. Journal writing has the potential to deepen our understanding of such 'messes'.

Portrait 6: The learning journal as: 'A means of searching for the truth'

Each journal entry should not be viewed as some absolute, fixed and verifiable truth. The last and final word on the clinical matter under consideration. In our value-laden practice worlds, truths are often partial, contested, intersubjective and illusive. It is through the journal writing process that we can come to appreciate our own perhaps altering views and the opinions that others hold about the same clinical phenomenon.

Portrait 7: The learning journal as: 'A basis for building a better world'

Journals should have a prospective quality. Constructive and critical reflections on past events should constitute a new beginning or an action plan to improve what is already being experienced and in existence. Journal writing interpreted in this way is situated in the realm of the good.

When do I write my learning journal?

You should aim to write regularly and at least once each week. Learning has to be given a chance to emerge so you need to make a series of entries and then re-read them to search for patterns, themes, issues, conflicts and so on. It is often useful to keep a small notebook to jot down the essence of interesting, satisfying, worrying and/or puzzling encounters and conversations as you go through the week. You can then elaborate upon them in your learning journal later.

What are the ethical implications of keeping a learning journal?

If health care is about helping clients with ethically laden health issues and decisions and if we caricature it as being interlaced with ethical dilemmas arising from practice (Bowman, 1994) then it is not surprising that enhancing learning through journal writing implies cognitive activity but also the need to embrace the process as a moral and ethical enterprise. Moving thinking and clinical practice forward requires not only expertise and commitment but also honesty and integrity. Put in its simplest form, ethics is about issues of right and wrong and good and bad (Burnard and Morrison, 1994; Burnard and Chapman, 1993). But ethics is a complex field, and in the context of learning journals we are lured into considerations of rationality, reason, 'right action', fairness, justice, equality, reciprocity and rules. We have grouped the ethical issues associated with journal writing under three headings. These are rights, risks and benefits, and consent.

The issue of rights

If you reflect on your practice through your learning journal you have certain rights. These relate to ideas of self-respect, self-esteem and dignity. Whether or not you keep your journal entries to yourself or share them in some way, you have the right to self-determination. You should not be coerced into making public what is written in your journal. You have the right to privacy. You should be the one who determines the time, extent and context under which you disclose your journal entries. You have the right to decide what you withhold and what you share. You also have the right to assume that the content of the entries you make public will be kept confidential. If you share the contents of your journal with others it is important that you get this issue of rights sorted out early on.

The issue of risks and benefits

In keeping a learning journal, feelings of discomfort and vulnerability may arise because you are asking yourself questions like, 'Why is my clinical practice like this?', 'How did it come to be this way?' and 'How can I improve it?'. A commitment to learn from journal writing is a commitment to a great deal of introspection, honesty with self, and a frame of mind that will be able to handle what you come to know in a constructive way. Sharing your journal entries with others may also put at risk such things as your level of self-confidence, call into question aspects of your practice and challenge your much cherished professional values. There are also risks for those who support or facilitate reflection through journal writing, like nurse educators, mentors and preceptors. What should or must they do for example if they hear an account of malpractice or care which the facilitator would consider as unsafe? What happens to notions of trust and confidentiality between people in such circumstances? Who becomes vulnerable, perhaps marginalised or peripheralised? Questions such as 'How far is the account true?', 'How far are we sure of it?' and 'What are the risks associated with not being sure?' need to be asked and responded to (Theobold, 1995).

The issue of consent

It is important to think through this issue if you are drawing upon the experiences of colleagues, in your learning journal, as a means to further your own ends. If journal entries are made public and shared for example with peers, issues about who is telling what, to whom and why, need to be sorted out. Additionally, the general dialogical environment needs to be supportive of this activity and requires some warmth and collective engagement. In listening to another's account we are given an entrée into someone else's clinical world. In disclosing what is in a learning journal, the 'teller' needs to be sure that they can trust others with what may be a sensitive, but certainly professionally significant, issue.

What are some of the 'tensions' that need to be resolved in keeping a learning journal?

Earlier we said that a learning journal was comprised of both a content and a process. Now we want to introduce you to the fact that these two elements are held in a 'tensioned' relationship. Some of the most important tensions that need resolving are described below.

Tension 1: Between writing personal and safe responses

The former is about content. It concerns that which is personally significant to you. The latter combines content with process. It wraps up concerns with what you write about with the way in which you write it. Developing your professionality through journal writing requires the development of an ability to write what you feel needs writing in a fair, accurate and honest manner and often to say things in a critical yet constructive way. Sometimes safe responses are written in a context of fear, dread and blame. Sometimes they are written up in a way so that they would not offend if they were to enter the public domain in some way.

Tension 2: Between nurse-centric and 'significant other' perspectives

This is about using the journal to present your view of things and your ability and preparedness to be open to the views of others. No account is free from bias and an amount of distortion (wilful or unconscious). No account is neutral and impartial. The journal can be used to represent alternative perspectives that allow you to see the same clinical phenomenon in different ways (Cooper, 1989). It can serve to illuminate the subjective connections of self with significant others (e.g. clients, managers, tutors).

Tension 3: Between privacy and the right to know

This is a complex and very 'contested' issue. We have said that you have the right to keep the contents of a learning journal private if you so wish. But this raises the moral problem concerning the rights that others have to know the content of your journal. Some of these rights are to do with journal writing in a context of professional and organisational accountability. Other rights are more legalistic in kind and relate to the way in which evidence from a journal might be used in a process of litigation. Then there is the right that some might exercise in terms of 'I have the right to know what it is you are writing about me!'. This is about the right to know and the right to intervene in the light of that information. Rights are problematic because they often contain appeals to different political, professional and moral values (Pring, 1988).

Tension 4: Between structure and freedom

Sometimes, if keeping a learning journal is a pre- or post-registration course requirement, expectations are raised about how far there is a predetermined structure or format for each entry. Whereas critical incident analysis can be enhanced by certain structured ways of looking at and learning from clinical experiences, keeping a learning journal offers health carers the freedom to express themselves in whatever style they choose, unfettered by 'academic' conventions and traditions. In reality, a compromise is reached between structuring an entry and the freedom to be creative.

Tension 5: Between the particular and the general

One journal entry is an account of a particular instance of practice, an encounter, a dialogue, a feeling, an achievement and so on. It is dangerous to read too much into one entry. Journals that contain numerous entries over time provide the potential for generalisation. This might be a generalisation about a personally preferred value position in relation to client care, about a usual way of providing an aspect of care, about a general strategy for managing the business of a ward and so on. In this sense 'general' means what you tend to generally do, think and feel. It may or may not be generally true for others. It is important to appreciate the difference between what is generally the case for you and what is not. In reflecting on your journal entries it is also important to try to tease out and establish what is particular and different in certain clinical contexts and what are the more patterned, regular and therefore more general things. If you make these general things known to others, such as peers and work colleagues, you give them the opportunity to generalise from them to their own clinical situation. This is called naturalistic generalisation (Stake, 1995).

Tension 6: Between dialogue and disillusionment

In some health care contexts extracts from learning journals are shared between peers and with tutors. This is justified on the grounds that learning accrues from the public articulation of the clinical issue and from the dialogue that it generates. The individual has to experience a benefit which might be in terms of new perspectives and insights offered by others on 'their issue'. Meaningful dialogues, whether in verbal or written form, about what has been articulated have to take the individual forward. This sense of moving forward will often be defined in very personal ways. Without this sense, dialogues of this kind can quickly lead to disillusionment and to feelings that the process was a 'waste of time'.

What are some of the common problems in keeping a learning journal?

Throughout this chapter we have been addressing some of the problems associated with learning journals, particularly with their purposes, content and form and the ethical issues that arise from these three things. We want to add four more problems drawn from the work of Paterson (1995) and then leave you, the reader, to weigh up and to counter-balance the pros and cons of learning through journal writing. They are:

1. **The problem of procrastination**: particularly if it is felt that keeping a learning journal is unworthy of the attention that course work assignments/exams deserve.
2. **The problem of superficial and unreflective entries**: there is no virtue in trying to describe and faithfully regurgitate what has happened to you. The idea is to set out the clinical phenomenon and then to interrogate it through the processes of writing, critical reflection and (in some cases) peer or collegial discussion.
3. **The problem of waning enthusiasm**: To make learning happen it needs to have a chance to take hold and be apprehended. It may help to view the learning journal as a companion, and to be committed to making regular entries and re-reading them over time.
4. **Unwillingness or inability to reflect**: As we have said earlier, reflection-on-practice is not just a cognitive activity but a moral, affective and ethical art form. You need to read about keeping a learning journal, about reflection being a specialised form of thinking and about learning being a complex activity.

In what ways can keeping a journal enhance learning?

The learning journal offers a learning experience in several senses. First, there is the opportunity for health carers to learn more about a substantive aspect of their clinical practice and the organisational culture in which it is embedded. For example, through the journal a nurse might learn more about caring for the elderly, about how to maximise the therapeutic potential of nursing, the rights of the unborn child, effective multidisciplinary team leadership and so on. Secondly, journal writing offers the opportunity to learn about the process of researching clinical practice, what questions to ask, what evidence to gather and what valid claims can be made about improvements in practice. Thirdly, journal writing offers an opportunity to learn about ourselves, about the kind of health care professional we are and wish to be.

For some health care professionals many benefits are claimed from the process of journal writing. In reviewing recent literature the benefits appear to cluster around three domains. Although it is difficult to categorise many of the articles on journal writing, the following have something significant to say about the domain with which they have been linked.

1. **Benefits in the cognitive domain**: about developing specific thinking skills like analysis, evaluation and critical thinking. See, for example, Hahnemann (1986) and Callister (1993).
2. **Benefits in the affective domain**: about feelings, attitudes, emotionality, self-concept, confidence and self-esteem. See, for example, Landeen *et al.* (1995).
3. **Benefits in the clinical action/competency domain**: about practical skills, technical competence, strengths and weaknesses. See, for example, Wallace (1996) and Burnard (1988).

The interesting question that arises from this review is 'Why do so few papers refer explicitly to the link between the benefits of journal writing and the *organisational domain*?'. One explanation perhaps resides in the commonly held humanistic view that journal writing is essentially a personal activity, for generating self-knowledge that leads to a more enlightened health care professional. This view is associated with professional development residing primarily in the worlds of the technical and the practical. If more was done by nurse educators and others to connect journal writing with critical social theory, the work of Habermas (1971) and emancipatory knowing, then perhaps the role of journal writing, which enables health carers to tackle the socio-cultural and politico-economic structures which constrain their lives, could be more widely known and appreciated. Recent research (Graham, 1994, p. 235) seems to clearly point us in this direction, particularly when he writes about:

> ... the often vulnerable and stressed position nurses find themselves in today when trying to meet their professional aspirations within a medically dominated, bureaucratic health-care system.

In our own work, both with nursing students and in particular with those undertaking a mentor and assessor course, the claims made as a consequence of keeping learning journals are most frequently related to the following:

Claim 1 'It can illuminate my thinking': anxieties, prejudices, partial knowledge, mental blocks

Claim 2 'It can show me how open and receptive I am': self-disclosure, openness, other points of view

Claim 3 'I can see how my thinking changes': altered appreciations, changing value positions

Claim 4 'It helps me to appreciate my general attitude to work': what I need to work at and improve, my future agenda

Claim 5 'It helps me get better at what I do': positive impact on clinical action and the quality of care

Claim 6 'It helps me in my advocacy role': more able to argue for resources, justify my practice to others, speak on behalf of others

Claim 7 'It was motivating': fun to do, compelling once patterns began to emerge, a different thing to do

References

Ackoff, R. (1979) The future of operational research is past. *Journal of Operational Research Society*, **30**, 93–104.

Ballantyne, R. and Packer, J. (1995) *Making Connections: Using Student Journals as a Teaching/Learning Aid*, Unpublished paper, School of Professional Studies, Faculty of Education, Queensland University of Technology, Brisbane, Australia.

Berger, P. and Luckmann, T. (1976) *The Social Construction of Reality*. Penguin, Harmondsworth.

Boud, D. (1996) *Enhancing Learning through Self Assessment*. Kogan Page, London.

Bowman, A. (1994) Teaching ethics: telling stories. *Nurse Education Today*, **15**(1), 33–8.

Burnard, P. (1988) The journal as an assessment and evaluation tool in nurse education. *Nurse Education Today*, **8**, 105–7.

Burnard, P. and Chapman, C. (1993) *Professional and Ethical Issues in Nursing: The Code of Professional Conduct*, 2nd edn, Scutari, Chichester.

Burnard, P. and Morrison, P. (1994) *Nursing Research in Action: Developing Basic Skills*. Macmillan Press, London.

Callister, L. (1993) The use of student journals in nursing education: making meaning out of clinical experience. *Journal of Nursing Education*, **32**(4), 185–6.

Cooper, M. (1989) Gilligan's different voice: a perspective for nursing. *Journal of Professional Nursing*, **5**(1), 10–16.

Department of Health (1989a) *Education and Training; Working Paper Ten*. HMSO, London.

Department of Health (1989b) *Working for Patients*. HMSO, London.

Department of Health (1993) *A Vision for the Future*. NHS Management Executive, London.

Department of Health (2004) *The NHS Knowledge and Skills Framework (NHS KSF) and the Development Review Process*. HMSO, London.

English National Board (1991) *Framework for Continuing Professional Education for Nursing, Midwifery and Health Visiting: Guide to Implementation*. English National Board, London.

English National Board (1994) *Creating Lifelong Learners: Partnerships for Care*. English National Board, London.

Ghaye, T. *et al.* (1996a) *Theory–Practice Relationships: Reconstructing Practice*. Formword Publications, Newcastle-upon-Tyne.

Ghaye, T. *et al.* (1996b) *Professional Values: Being a Professional*. Formword Publications, Newcastle-upon-Tyne.

Graham, I. (1994) How do registered nurses think and experience nursing?: A phenomenological investigation. *Journal of Clinical Nursing*, **3**, 235–42.

Guba, E. and Lincoln, Y. (1989) *Fourth Generation Evaluation*. Sage Publications, London.

Habermas, J. (1971) *Knowledge and Human Interests*. Beacon, Boston.

Hahnemann, B. (1986) Journal writing: a key to promoting critical thinking in nursing students. *Journal of Nursing Education*, **25**, 213–15.

Holly, M. (1987) *Keeping a Personal-Professional Journal*. Deakin University Press, Victoria.

Holly, M. (1989) *Writing to Grow: Keeping a Personal-Professional Journal*. Heinemann, Portsmouth, NH.

Landeen, J. *et al.* (1995) Exploring the lived experiences of psychiatric nursing students through self-reflective journals. *Journal of Advanced Nursing*, **21**, 878–85,

McNiff, J. (1990) Writing and the creation of educational knowledge. In: *Managing Staff Development in Schools* (ed. P. Lomax). Multi-Lingual Matters, Clevedon.

Paterson, B. (1995) Developing and maintaining reflection in clinical journals. *Nurse Education Today*, **15**, 211–20.

Pring, R. (1988) Confidentiality and the right to know. In: *Evaluating Education: Issues and Methods* (eds. R. Murphy and H. Torrance). Paul Chapman, London.

Stake, R. (1995) *The Art of Case Study Research*. Sage Publications, London.

Theobold, M. (1995) *The Nature of Nursing Knowledge*. Keynote speech at the Conference on Reflective Practice: The Impact on Patient Care. Commonwealth Institute, London.

Thomas, D. (1992) *Putting Nature to the Rack: Narrative Studies as Research*. Paper presented at the Teachers' Stories of Life and Work Conference, Chester, UK.

Thorpe, K. (2004) Reflective learning journals: from concept to practice. *Reflective Practice*, **5**(3), 327–43.

Wallace, D. (1996) Using reflective diaries to assess students. *Nursing Standard*, **10**(36), 44–7.

CHAPTER 4

Examples of journal writing

In Chapter 3 we raised the question, 'What do I put into a learning journal?'. In this chapter we have included some examples of the different ways health care professionals have made their journal entries. Above all other things, each entry must be:

- concerned with something professionally significant
- written or entered in your journal in such a way that it makes sense to you

There is no real virtue in trying to follow some notion of 'academic convention' each time you use your journal. You must create the kind of 'text' that we described earlier. This is a 'text' that you can learn from. There are no 'writing rules'. You should let go of any notions that you have of trying to 'get it right first time'. The personal relevance and meaningfulness of your journal entries are important qualities. So in keeping a journal you should not get bogged down with issues of 'better' or 'worse', about writing better, tighter, more economically, having more control of words and so on because this begs the tricky question 'What constitutes better?'. More important things are trying to create entries which allow you to search for new angles on professional concerns, biases, fragmented and woolly thinking, new juxtapositions and important associations that perhaps had remained unknown to you and been uncelebrated. It is also important to avoid the 'paralysis by analysis syndrome'. Be patient and realistic with what you want to get out of your journal writing. It is unrealistic to think that new and wonderful clinical insights will emerge, as if by magic, from one or two short entries!

In making an entry, what you focus upon and how you record it in your journal are two things that need to be thought through. For example in making a conscious decision to focus upon those aspects of your work that are professionally significant, you may focus upon one thing such as your 'decision making', or your 'interpersonal skills' or your ability to 'develop shared beliefs and understandings' within a team. Alternatively, you may feel that you want to focus upon lots of different things that are professionally significant. Both approaches are legitimate. Both have two things in common. First you need to create a number of 'texts'. That is to say, you need to make multiple entries, over time. This relates to the issue of giving yourself a chance to let the 'problematics' of your clinical practice come to the surface. Secondly, the texts you create need to be interrogated at a later date. It is through this process of interrogation that learning from reflection-on-practice can begin to take hold. In keeping a learning journal there must be a commitment on your part to return to the 'texts' you have created and to learn from them. Learning arises from the re-exploration of past experiences. You may get caught up in the swirl of so many things that you might give your attention to. A more unified, consistent and holistic understanding of practice can be a struggle, but it should be your goal.

In this chapter we identify six examples of 'types of journal entry'. Each type represents a different way of representing what the health carer wanted to record in the journal. Sometimes a series of entries in your journal might be in the same form. But there is no reason why you should not change the form of your entry in the same way that you might change the focus of it. One entry might also embrace more than one form. The 'types of journal entry' that are most often used we have labelled thus:

- Faithful regurgitation type
- Off-load type
- Extend and revise type
- Concept mapping type
- Knotty and messy type
- Living contradiction type

What follows are some examples of each type. In publishing these we have had to be mindful of the issues of consent and confidentiality. We have sampled from a range of types of entry. We have also had permission to edit each one so that their main characteristic comes through clearly. However, there is a natural blurring of the edges between types.

Example 1: The faithful regurgitation type

The emphasis in entries of this kind is upon 'what I've done'. They tend to be mainly descriptive and can be written up in a vivid manner. There is a reflective component and sometimes an evaluative dimension. There is often an initial anxiety in relation to 'Will this entry tell me anything later?'. There can also be problems with selection, detail and length of the entry. Sometimes the entry takes on the air of a pseudo- and mini-essay. Sometimes such entries contain references to the professional and/or medical literature. The example is from an experienced paediatric nurse who is keeping a journal as part of an award-bearing continuing professional development course. She has just spent the day in seminar work discussing HIV infection and AIDS in children.

> Well we started the day on time... thank goodness, because if we had started late again all the seminars would have got behind. Trudy and Julie gave the first presentation... they were really good, dynamic, confident... all the kinds of thing that I hoped mine would be. It's better I think if you do it together... but I drew the short straw so had to do it on my own. Trudy and Julie spoke a lot about the AMERICAN research. I couldn't believe that 1,500–2,000 HIV-infected infants can be expected to be born each year in the States! They finished well in talking about issues of vulnerability and dependency because of the nature of the disease and its social context.

> I was quite pleased with my presentation. I kept to time... 45 minutes is not enough though. I got through the things I wanted to say. I even used the overhead and got the acetates the right way around for a change! I made my three main points about children being infected with HIV through three main routes: (a) receipt of infected blood (b) sexual or drug use behaviours or (c) vertical transmission from an infected mother. It seemed to go all right. There weren't many questions at the end... but they did seem interested. I was quite nervous... and maybe I might have slowed down what I said. I think they got a bit over-loaded... they were interested though... I think!

Example 2: The off-load type

Entries of this kind tend to be high on emotionality, with the practitioner often claiming that the entry is 'personal and pertinent'. They frequently focus upon an encounter with significant others – often colleagues – and may contain disagreements over practice and/or policy. The entry is 'significant' in that it makes us cross, it will not go away, has not resolved itself or has questioned our professionality. Some entries of this type can be quite judgemental. The writing process can be carthartic. Through it we can purge ourselves of pent-up emotions (Holly, 1989). The example is from the journal of a nurse who is working with a psychiatric patient.

> Christ what a day... I sometimes wonder why I do this work. It's hard enough without all this. Why is it that he [the doctor] always treats me like an idiot? He knows best... he just doesn't seem to listen. It's not that I am questioning his ability or even his judgement... but I do know Jim [the patient]... I know him bloody well. Jim has been telling me that he feels that the drugs are making him feel unwell... he has said this for some time. I try to tell the doctor this but he thinks that Jim's condition will get worse if the drugs are discontinued. All I want is to be taken seriously... I don't feel that I am being listened to. I can't seem to speak to the doctor in the right way. I CAN'T FIND THE RIGHT REPLY TO WHAT THAT PERSON SAYS!! Jim can't argue for himself so I've got to do it for him. Jim has rights... I have rights... why won't he seem to listen?

Example 3: The extend and revise type

This type can only be found in journals where the practitioner has made a number of entries and arises from revisiting, reviewing and re-appreciating earlier entries. It is evidence of a systematic and committed approach to reflect-on-practice. With entries of this kind there is an opportunity to do a number of things, such as:

(a) celebrate the good and rewarding aspects of practice
(b) continue to moan about the bad bits of your work
(c) re-relieve yourself of any feelings of frustration
(d) remind yourself of the things that you had forgotten
(e) re-examine earlier responses to significant incidents
(f) look again for beliefs, prejudices and those things that get in the way of moving your practice forward
(g) separate out in your head those things that you have some control over and can influence from those that you presently cannot.
(h) take stock of 'where you are at'

In adopting this style it is important to date each entry. In this way you will be able to place altered or confirmed thoughts, feelings and actions on a time line. This temporal dimension to your journal entries might give you a way in to understanding more richly notions of professional 'development'. The example is drawn from the journal of a nurse who is working with children with profound and multiple learning difficulties. Early in her journal she develops some 'brief sketches' of the children with whom she works most closely.

Date: September

John

Aged 9. John sits quietly and passively in his wheelchair. He 'comes alive' when placed on the floor, moving about by lively actions which are neither rolling nor crawling. John is unable to travel in any particular direction and has no sense of danger and therefore wears a safety helmet. He cannot walk. John does not appear to use gesture of any sort to indicate his understanding or needs and cannot speak. He often appears impervious to stimulation but occasionally shows real pleasure by looking intently at some wind-chimes or some disco-type lighting. John is unable to feed himself and is doubly incontinent and severely epileptic.

James

James is 9 and cortically blind but walks with help and splashes around the swimming pool with armbands. James can communicate and although his speech is limited and repetitive he makes relationships with his carers. James needs... and demands... a great deal of attention. He explores the environment with his hands but is unaware of his own strength, cheerfully destroying playthings. James needs help to feed himself with a spoon. He is doubly incontinent and epileptic.

Jayne

7 years old and unable to speak, Jayne often looks around at everything and everyone with interest. She has a beautiful smile and is able to communicate to a very limited degree by facial expressions and sounds. Jayne is unable to walk. She has difficulty in using her hands but enjoys being helped to play with toys. Jayne is at the early stages of learning to feed herself. She is incontinent.

Date: May the next year

These sketches of the children were among the first entries in my journal... the first pieces of reflective writing. I have often read them over but always uncritically. But now I am returning to them with some distress. I feel the descriptions are negative and mechanistic.... The terms used reflect my deep steeping in medical models of care and negative attitudes towards children with PMLD. On reflection the sketches are an unfortunate entrée to my journal. The following is a second attempt at James' sketch:

James is a handsome boy from a very warm and loving family. Despite blindness and disabilities due to an early childhood illness he has learned to speak. He frequently delights us with things that he says (often single words) which show that he has understood the situation. He has a wicked sense of fun and a 'party spirit'. When working with James you have to be careful not to let him know you would like him to do X. It is better to approach things in a 'sidelong' manner or he will insist on doing Y instead, usually grinning as he does so! James has an attractive personality which people 'take to' and therefore he generally gets plenty of attention... which he thrives on. James enjoys himself a lot and gives pleasure to many people.

This sketch offers, I think, a more rounded 'human' picture. It provides a vivid contrast to my earlier writing particularly as I've decided to write on the opposite page. Again, however, the picture is limited and distorted compared with the full complexity of this child. It also seems fairly patronising and does not attempt a look at James' views on the world. This in turn may say quite a lot about my world view! These are issues I will need to explore later in my journal.

Example 4: The concept mapping type

Entries of this type are increasing in popularity. They are more pictorial or 'graphical' than literary. A concept map contains health care knowledge which is represented in the form of a labelled-line graph structure in which the three fundamental elements are:

■ Nodes: key ideas or concepts
■ Links: lines drawn between the nodes
■ Relations: the meaning given to the nodes by the nature of the links between them.

In essence, concept maps, as journal entries, are personal reality maps, constructed by you, to express the sense or meaning you currently have of a particular facet of your health care work. They are your subjective construction of an aspect of your world. If your journal contains a number of maps which focus on the same area or issue, then learning can arise because their analysis can reveal how:

■ You might fine tune your 'know that', 'know how' and 'know why' knowledge
■ Far ideas remain isolated or more integrated and structured in your mind
■ You may have changed your perception of aspects of your practice over time

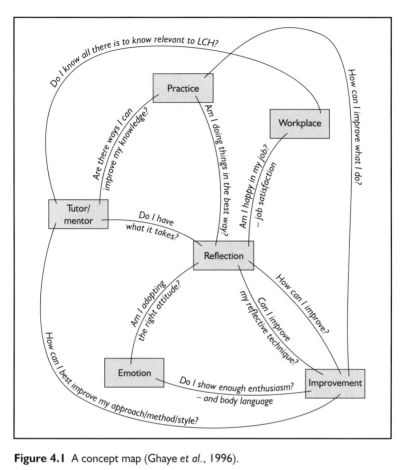

Figure 4.1 A concept map (Ghaye *et al.*, 1996).

Figure 4.1 shows an example of a concept map where a practitioner is reflecting upon some of the 'building blocks' for professional development. Notice how she has placed 'reflection' in the centre of her map and the questioning tone that the map conveys.

Example 5: The knotty and messy type

'Knots' have been described by Wagner (1987) as the interrelationship between cognitive and affective processes which lead to conflict and professional dilemmas. Drawing upon theories in cognitive psychology, clinical psychology and psychotherapy, she identifies six types of conflict or 'knot', some of which might be short-lived, while others might last for years. What each type of 'knot' has in common is that they arise due to a discrepancy or dilemma between 'what is' and 'what must or should be'. Ackoff (1979) uses the notion of 'messes' to express a similar kind of thing. In our everyday clinical practice our thinking often gets snarled up in a 'knot'. Knots can affect our clinical action. Sometimes we react to knots by complaining. Knots need tackling. The example is drawn from the journal of an experienced neonatal nurse who has been given the role of establishing a 'nursing development unit' (NDU). The 'knot' is centrally about redefining and clarifying roles.

> I really feel under some pressure. I'm still not sure of my role... it's blurring a lot with that of ward sister. I'm not sure how far I should keep some clinical involvement, retreat from ward activity... just get on with the strategic and business bit. I feel pretty screwed up right now because I haven't resolved how I should... or must... try to balance clinical care with my managerial responsibilities. I want to avoid being too 'distant' though.... I guess I've got to sort out some kind of balance between my clinical and developmental commitments. I can speak the language of clinical practice but can I speak the language of management sufficiently well?... It's something I've got to unravel and sort out.

Example 6: The living contradiction type

Journal entries of this type acknowledge that clinical practice is a value-laden activity. The entries focus upon the nature of the professional values that give clinical practice its shape, form and purpose. A prerequisite for being able to write entries of this kind is knowing your professional values. The entry then focuses upon how far you are able to live out your values in your practice. The extent to which you are able to do this and support such a claim is an important entry to make. It is also important to record those things which enable and facilitate this process and also the impediments. Additionally, there is an opportunity for you to focus your attention on the 'contradictions' (Whitehead, 1994) in your clinical work. A contradiction can be an occasion on which we say one thing and yet act in a manner which is inconsistent and which contradicts that espoused value position. If we take Whitehead's suggestion to consider ourselves as 'living contradictions' we can write about these, over time, and regard them as professional growth points. It is not a question of trying to eradicate all contradictions from our practice – our professional lives are not as straightforward as this. With some contradictions we may have to say to ourselves: 'Well, I've been exploring this through my journal writing for some time now, and I've come to the conclusion that that's how it is and there isn't a great deal I can do about things for the time being'. The examples are drawn from a number of individual journals from nurses and midwives. They all reflect contradictions between what people say and do.

> I believe that a patient's quality of life is the most important consideration, and yet I use sophisticated technology which prolongs a life which has no future, purpose and happiness, and more suffering is caused by a continuance.

> I believe that I should always take the time and care to answer patient's questions fully and unhurriedly, and yet due to the pressure of being a ward co-ordinator I am not always able to do this.

> I believe that each patient that I am responsible for is worthy of my constant care and attention because each one has mental health problems unique to them and needs 'professional' attention… and yet… time and resources prevent this, resulting in nurses being involved in intensive care or crisis management with people with less 'risky/acute' problems taking a back seat.

> I believe parents should be allowed to stay with their children in our department at all times, but because some consultants do not allow this, I am always asking parents to go, so I am always in conflict. Parents have rights.

These examples of journal writing reflect the different ways in which health care professionals have tried to sharpen their perceptions of the everyday realities of their clinical work. Journal writing can help us to extend our understandings, insights and command of the clinical situations in which we work. These examples have shown that keeping a journal can help us to recognise contradictions of purpose and value. The examples represent authentic portrayals of clinical experience. They are 'realities' which need to be constructed, deconstructed, interrogated, critiqued and transformed over time. One nurse wrote about this process in a most vivid manner:

> … all the turning back and turning over, and again. I felt I was pushing myself into corners and forcing myself to stay there until I'd worked out a valid response or answer to things. And then it got worse as I took it more seriously. Back in the corners again, and this time instead of crawling around muttering, I felt I had to stand up and confront the corners. I did feel like bumping around in the dark. Then it began to dawn on me. I was refusing to see that it was me who had to

switch on the lights. And the switches... generally... were just above my head. In the end I found some interesting pictures in the corners and it made a real change from circling around in the middle of the room.

These examples emphasise the importance of concentrating on particularity and our everyday clinical experiences in our search for new knowledge, understandings and sensitivities. In turning to the new science of chaos we find ample support for this belief (Gleick, 1988, p. 8):

> The modern study of chaos began with the creeping realization in the 1960s that quite simple mathematical equations could model systems every bit as violent as a waterfall. Tiny differences in input could quickly become overwhelming differences in output.... In weather, for example, this translates into what is only half-jokingly known as the Butterfly Effect – the notion that a butterfly stirring the air today in Peking can transform storm systems next month in New York.

The entries we place in our learning journals are knowledge encapsulated in particularity. In the stirrings of these butterfly wings we have the starting point for transforming our understanding about the nature of our professionalism and for improving the quality of client care.

References

Ackoff, R. (1979) The future of operational research is past. *Journal of Operational Research Society*, **30**, 93–104.

Ghaye, T. (1996) *Professional Values: Being a Professional*. Pentaxion Press, Newcastle Upon Tyne.

Gleick, J. (1988) *Chaos: Making a New Science*. Heinemann, London.

Holly, M. (1989) *Writing to Grow: Keeping a Personal-Professional Journal*. Heinemann, Portsmouth, NH.

Wagner, A. (1987) 'Knots' in teachers' thinking. In: *Exploring Teachers' Thinking* (ed. J. Calderhead). Cassell, London.

Whitehead, J. (1994) *Creating Living Educational Theory*. Hyde Publications, Bournemouth.

CHAPTER 5

Critical incident analysis

Minghella and Benson (1995) identify that critical incident analysis has been espoused as a valuable method of promoting reflective practice in health care, and can be used as a tool in developing curriculum content. Benner (1984) also notes the use of critical incident analysis and its assistance in attaining *competence* in nursing skills and the development of the *'expert practitioner'*. Powell (1989) noted that experienced practice is not wholly dependent upon the time spent in the job; therefore the experience has to be gained through some other process. Critical incident analysis can be used as one of those processes that assist the individual in becoming an experienced practitioner.

In this chapter we will attempt to explore the use and value of critical incident analysis and its identification of learning through experience, thereby moving forward the professional boundaries and promoting 'good' practice.

Critical incident analysis may also be used as a tool to develop and identify reflective practice for the individual, providing them with a means of keeping records of evidence for the individual practitioner's personal professional profile, and so fulfilling part of the PREP, KSF and other professional requirements.

It is advocated by Parker *et al.* (1995) that through critical incidents the development of knowledge, skills and *attitudes* is grounded in practice through the process of reflection-on-action. This chapter will also guide the individual practitioner in the identification and recording of critical incidents, discussing the value of *experiential learning* and gaining new knowledge through practice. The recording of these incidents may also act as a measure of the individual's practice fulfilling both the professional and governmental requirements of clinical practice discussed in Chapters 1 and 7.

Where do critical incidents come from?

John Flannagan (1954), an aviation psychologist with the United States Air Force, developed the procedure for gathering information concerning effective and ineffective behaviour in certain situations. The combat veterans that he was studying reported incidents which they considered either helpful or inadequate in accomplishing a designated mission. Flannagan produced a focused description that provided a systematic, open-ended procedure for obtaining data in both verbal and written formats. He then analysed these incidents and produced a list of critical behaviours for the performance of tasks. It was Benner (1984) who primarily introduced the idea into nursing and suggested that it could assist in the development of expertise in practice. Using critical incidents, Benner suggested that, over a period of time, following exposure to theory and reflection on the application of critical incidents to clinical practice, the concept would assist the individual practitioner to develop into what she refers to as an 'expert practitioner'. Benner noted that the theory taught in the basic training of nurses offered knowledge that can be made explicit and formalised; this is the scientific knowledge described by Carper (1978). Benner refers to it as concrete theory or the science of nursing. However, clinical practice, she notes, is more complex and presents many more realities for the individual practitioner than can be captured by scientific knowledge alone. Benner noted that what she refers to as the 'expert practitioner' can be influenced through this process, providing positive outcomes for the practitioner's clients. Clinical knowledge, argues Schon (1987) develops as practical experience which is combined with the application of theoretical knowledge and is further redefined and extended with practice. Schon (1983) recommended reflection on critical incidents as a valuable learning tool. Flannagan's critical incident technique has also been used in health care to elicit indicators of high and low quality of patient care (Norman *et al.*, 1992). Critical incidents may then assist individual practitioners in drawing on their experience, helping them to make sense of those experiences, facilitating learning through them and allowing them to utilise their scientific knowledge applying it to clinical practice. Chesney (1996) argues that reflecting on past experiences and making sense of them assists in the application of theory to practice, this being scientific knowledge applied to clinical practice.

What are critical incidents?

Tripp (1993, p. 8) defines critical incidents as:

incidents happen, but critical incidents are produced by the way we look at a situation, it is an interpretation of the significance of the event.

Clamp (1980, p. 1756) describes them as:

Snapshot views of daily work of the nurse and by examining them the effects of care on patients can be seen, and interactions between colleagues can be highlighted.

Critical incidents then are not just the experiences we all live through, but are the experiences we analyse and use to identify *aesthetic* knowledge and the *experiential learning* acquired. It is the analysis and evaluation of the experience that can then be used to improve clinical practice, apply scientific knowledge and ultimately develop and provide evidence of an 'expert practitioner'.

In the health care arena the word 'critical' often conjures up an experience that has had some major implications for our practice or an incident of an emergency nature, e.g. cardiac arrest or drug error. Although these situations can be used as critical incidents and learning experiences they are not the only experiences that can be used. Any experience that the individual encounters is potentially a critical incident, and therefore a situation the individual can reflect upon.

The actual incident can then be:

- An incident that is an ordinary experience.
- An incident where the experience did not go to plan (these may be positive as well as negative experiences),
- An incident that went well.
- An incident that reflects the values and beliefs held by the individual.
- An incident that identifies the contribution of qualified practitioners.
- An incident that allows the identification of learning.

Minghella and Benson (1995) note in their study that most incidents appear to represent interpersonal or interactional situations rather than clinical procedural problems. The latter also represent a valuable tool to identify our practice.

It is the reflection on these incidents and the analysis of these that assist practitioners in moving their practice forward and obtaining the expert nurse status.

How to find an incident

We experience new and repeated incidents every day of our lives, and the practice we now perform has often been learned from previous experiences. The problem with this experiential learning so far is that it has not been at a conscious level or recorded in any form, as required for continuing professional development. So how do we identify an incident for ourselves that will demonstrate our professional knowledge and competence and assist in providing a good quality of care to our clients?

Some of these incidents can be drawn from past experiences where the experience made an impact on our practice:

As a student I remember my first death. This was a critical incident that some 18 years later I can remember vividly. The situation was on a care of the elderly ward and I was to assist the qualified nurse in the laying out procedure. The nurse explained what we were to do and allowed me to talk through the procedure before going in to the patient. The two of us then proceeded to lay the patient out, maintaining dignity and respect for the deceased. Following the procedure the nurse again talked through what we had done and my feelings related to the task. This incident is still recalled as I review my own approach to the laying out of clients; the way I was treated had influenced how I wanted to assist individuals in their first encounters with the dead patient. It was a positive incident that I could reflect upon and so inform my practice, through the experience learning together with the scientific knowledge taught in the classroom. This provided me with an example of good nursing practice.

Equally, these experiences happen to us in our current practice and can have as just much effect on the way we deliver our care. Alternatively on the way home from work we often think back on the days activities and the situations that have arisen, how we dealt with them, these can be as important to our practice as the major events, and if recorded will provide a rich source of reflection that can then be consciously analysed.

Recording these incidents is important. The longer they are left the less easy it is to record the detail necessary to conduct a proper evaluation of them. They may initially be recorded in the learning journal as discussed in Chapters 3 and 4.

How to analyse the incident

These incidents can be used to offer a starting point for self-examination of our values, beliefs and self-understanding, as well as written evidence for the professional requirements. Tripp (1993) suggests that in analysing these events we may be able to verify something we suspected, or reveal something entirely new.

Tripp identifies five methods of analysing the incidents:

- Thinking strategies
- The Why? challenge
- Dilemma identification
- Personal theory analysis
- Ideology critique

Thinking strategies

Tripp (1993) uses certain thinking strategies to assist in the analysis of the identified incident. He suggests that framing questions about the incidents can lead us to a deeper reading or seeking of scientific knowledge on the subject encountered. The care of the patient with a new condition or the administration of a new drug could be overlooked by a practitioner if they were merely to look after the patient, the thinking strategy analysing their practice will provide the individual with the ability of seeking further scientific and other types of knowledge that may then have an effect on the care that they administer.

Tripp (1993) also suggests that this thinking strategy should take the form of reviewing the non-event: in other words, what did not happen. If a situation went well it is not in our nature to question or to think about it again. In this analysis Tripp suggests that we review what may have happened rather than continuing our practice blindly. What if it had happened in a different way? It might have been better, or if something had not happened how can we be assured that it was not just chance that occurred? To continue good practice we need also to reflect on the positive incidents and the things to celebrate in our practice. These are just as 'critical' and need to be nourished. Looking at practice and the same situation from other points of view, utilising the knowledge that we have gained over time, can sometimes illuminate different perspectives on the same aspect of care. These new ways of seeing may provide useful ways to take our practice forward.

The Why? challenge

If we continue to ask why-type questions of our practice, Tripp suggests that we will often end up with one of two answers. The first is, 'because that is how it ought to be'. This assists in recognising that we are operating from deeply held beliefs. For example, what if we ask 'Why do you wash the patient rather than letting them do it for themselves?'. Through an analysis of this it may be possible to identify the individual's belief in nursing that they are there to do this for the patients.

The second answer is often 'because that is how it is'. Tripp argues that this denotes something we take for granted and therefore feel we can not change.

> I remember when on the wards the patients' temperatures were taken every four hours even as they left to go home. If I had been asked why at the time, I probably would have replied in the above manner after justifying the importance of temperature taking and all the arguments that I could have thought of.

This approach, the Why? challenge, may lead us into exploring new alternatives or identifying areas for future practitioner research.

Dilemma identification

This is another useful way to make sense of practice. Our clinical work is full of dilemmas. They often evidence themselves as mismatches between what we say and do, think and feel, and between our values-in-practice and those of others. As one professional holds differing beliefs from another we can be faced with dilemmas in judgement or decision-making: for example, the doctor who does not want the patient to know their diagnosis against the patient who trusts in you and asks what is wrong with them. Where do we go for help? Who are we accountable to? What about the nurse's professional judgement? How do these incidents provide a means of learning from and promotion of 'good practice'? The first step is to recognise and appreciate that there is a dilemma present in our practice. Once this has been identified the process of critical reflection and meaning-making can begin.

Personal theory analysis

Here Tripp argues that we need to articulate our set of beliefs that inform our professional judgement and thereby our action in the material world, e.g. do we believe 'nursing' is doing for the patient or assisting the patient? Both beliefs will result in slightly different care being given to the clients. Choosing one solution over the other enables us to identify the values that we hold inherent in our professional judgement. Analysis may identify for us where our personal theory is grounded and therefore why we practice in the manner demonstrated.

Ideology critique

Tripp argues that this process has to do with the way in which certain ideas represent the world to us. This makes us behave and think in certain ways to legitimate what we do or have done to us by others and so provides a rationale for our behaviour. These ideas are more difficult to analyse than the specific and practice-based examples already given. Ideologies are big organising frameworks that have political, professional and personal aspects to them.

Recording critical incidents

There are several formats that can be used to record the process of critical incident analysis (Benner, 1984; Minghella and Benson, 1995; Lillyman

- ■ Description of the incident?
- ■ By whom was it handled?
- ■ What learning occurred?
- ■ What were the outcomes of this incident?
- ■ How has this incident affected your practice?

Figure 5.1 Critical incident analysis (Lillyman and Evans, 1996).

and Evans, 1996). The recording and analysing of these incidents can, for example, be used as evidence for the PREP requirements or KSF, at job interviews and to demonstrate learning through practice.

It is suggested that, for the purpose of the profile, the incident and analysis are limited to one side of A4 (see Figure 5.1) and that the description preserves the anonymity of those involved and the clinical context. The analysis should always stipulate the learning that has accrued and its application and relevance for practice. Chapter 6 provides a number of incidents that can be analysed in a variety of ways.

To recap, there are several reasons why critical incident analysis is useful to the practitioner.

1. As mentioned, it provides the evidence required for the practitioner to enter into their professional profile for PREP or practice development plan for KSF requirements, and provides evidence of professional development.
2. It can provide the individual with incidents of good practice that can be used during an interview to identify the interaction of theory with practice and/or how practice has been adapted, enriched and improved through reflection.
3. It provides the individual with written evidence and records of their professional development as they move through their career and gain more experiential knowledge through their practice.
4. It provides evidence of an ability to 'theorise' about practice, which is a quality needed for enrolment on award-bearing courses or to gain some accreditation of prior experiential learning.
5. It provides evidence which may help us to identify the reflective practitioner in the clinical environment.
6. It provides evidence of the unique contribution that health care professionals can make in the clinical situation.

7. The analysis of critical incidents can also be viewed as rich, contextual research data to add fuel to the argument that health care should be, and is, evidence-based.

Critical incident analysis is then primarily important for the individual practitioner to facilitate their professional development and identify and justify changes in their practice.

References

Benner, P. (1984) *From Novice to Expert*. Addison-Wesley, California.

Carper, B. (1978) Fundamental pattern of knowing. *Advances in Nursing Science*, **1**, 13–23.

Chesney, M. (1996) Sharing reflections on critical incidents in midwifery practice. *British Journal of Midwifery*, **4**(1), 8–10.

Clamp, C. (1980) Learning through incidents. *Nursing Times*, **76**(40), 1755–8.

Flannagan, J. (1954) The critical incident technique. *Psychological Bulletin*, **51**, 327–58.

Lillyman, S. and Evans, B. (1996) *Designing a Personal Portfolio/Profile*. Quay Books, Dinton.

Minghella, E. and Benson, A. (1995) Developing reflective practice in mental health nursing through critical incident analysis. *Journal of Advanced Nursing*, **21**, 205–13.

Norman, I., Redfern, S., Tomlin, D., and Oliver, S. (1992) Developing Flannagan's critical incident technique to elicit indicators of high and low quality nursing care. *Journal of Advanced Nursing*, **17**, 590–600.

Parker, D., Webb, J. and D'Souza, B. (1995) The value of critical incident analysis as an educational tool and its relationship to experiential learning. *Nurse Education Today*, **15**, 111–16.

Powell, J. (1989) The reflective practitioner in nursing. *Journal of Advanced Nursing*, **14**, 824–32.

Schon, D. (1983) *The Reflective Practitioner: How Practitioners Think in Action*. HarperCollins, San Francisco.

Schon, D. (1987) *Educating the Reflective Practitioner*. Jossey Bass, San Francisco.

Tripp, D. (1993) *Critical Incidents in Teaching*. Routledge, London.

CHAPTER 6

Examples of critical incident analysis

This chapter provides several examples of critical incident analysis identifying how and where these can be applied to clinical practice. The examples are provided as guidelines to help to identify learning and do not necessarily identify an expert practitioner. The incidents analysed in this chapter may be used in personal professional profiles as evidence of the development of expertise in clinical practice. They can identify where the *aesthetic* knowledge has been acquired through an individual's clinical practice and experience. Critical incident analysis recognises that learning occurs outside the formal boundaries of academic study and therefore promotes the idea of the health care professional as a *lifelong learner*.

Uses of critical incident analysis in personal profiles

Critical incident analysis can be used in various personal profiles that an individual practitioner will produces in their career. These include the profiles for:

■ Personal Development Plan within the NHS Knowledge and Skills Framework (KSF)
■ Post-Registration Education and Practice requirements (PREP)
■ Job interviews
■ Accreditation of prior experiential learning

Personal professional development

For all professionals the Knowledge and Skills Framework requirements (Department of Health, 2004) provide an ideal opportunity to
utilise critical incident analysis. These may be used in the personal professional profile to identify how individuals have maintained and developed their clinical competence. The analysis of the incident provides a
written format stating how personal and practice knowledge interacts
with the clinical context. Critical incident analysis can also be used as
a developmental measurement tool. Here individual practitioners can,
over time, measure their personal and professional development in
their clinical practice and identify where and how it has changed; for
example, it might be a situation that identifies how the individual deals
with an issue today compared with a similar experience earlier in their
career. The analysis may then include why their practice has changed
in relation to learning new scientific and *experiential* knowledge and
gaining expertise in their field of practice due to the introduction of new
policies and procedures.

Job interviews

Critical incident analysis can be used in preparation for a job interview.
When putting a profile together it is suggested that the profile reflects
the job description/person specification for the job. Individuals may then
draw on their experiences in practice to show how they dealt with a given
situation (see Example 1 below), identifying how theory and practice
interrelate.

Accreditation of prior experiential learning (APEL)

On entering courses or gaining accreditation for prior learning, the profile plays a valid part in the analysis and assessment of practice. Critical
incident analysis can be used here to reflect on the learning that has
occurred in clinical practice and how the individual has utilised theory
in their area of practice, identifying areas of *specialist and advanced
practice*.

Recording critical incidents

It is suggested that, when using critical incidents in profiles for job interviews and professional requirements, the incident analysis be limited to one side of A4. This will assist those reading it to gain an overview of the learning that has occurred. For APEL the word limit is usually set by the institution you are seeking accreditation with and guidelines must be gained from that institution prior to completing the profile.

Critical incident analysis used for job interviews

Example 1 identifies an incident analysed in such a way that it could be incorporated into a profile for a job interview. The incident discussed in this example was used for a job interview where the nurse was seeking to move from an adult to a paediatric oncology ward. Based on the job description, the individual would be expected to have some knowledge and experience of caring for a dying child and the support required for the whole family. This nurse, when applying for the post, did not have any first-hand experience specifically with the dying child, as all her experience to date was with the dying adult. Although some skills she noted were transferable from the care of the adult patient, the situation was somewhat different in contextual and emotional issues. As the nurse had no first-hand experience she reflected on her training, where she had worked on the paediatric wards, observing qualified practitioners who dealt with the dying child. The nurse described a situation that she had observed as a student. The incident was then analysed with the specific job description in mind for a specific interview.

When attending the interview the nurse was then able to discuss the incident and learning that occurred as she was questioned about her ability and skills in dealing with the dying child. She was not able, in this situation to use her own practice, but identified an area of what she perceived as good practice from the observation of the qualified nurse dealing with the situation. She then analysed the individual and noted why she perceived it as 'good' practice, informing the panel at the interview of what she had learned from her observations and how she would utilise the knowledge gained from her observations when facing the situation for herself.

Example 1: Critical incident analysis

Description of incident
Whilst working on a paediatric medical ward there were several occasions where I was able to observe a staff nurse and her approach to the dying child and relatives. Relationships with the patients and their family played an important part of the process. On the day the child died the staff nurse on duty allocated her time to the child, making sure that she was responsible for talking with the relatives, allowing them space and time to grieve and offering support without being over bearing.

By whom was it handled?
This incident was handled by the staff nurse, who had built up a relationship with the family and the patient. Each death where possible in this clinical area was handled in the same manner.

What learning occurred?
For me it was the building up of the relationship and the preparation for the expected death that played a major role in dealing with the situation. Supporting all involved throughout the illness and then following up. The grieving process could be identified in this situation from the time of diagnosis and observing the staff nurse as she recognised and supported the relatives through the various stages, even when stages of grief were repeated as the time went on.

What were the outcomes of the incident?
Observing an holistic approach for the patient and their family, and the importance of clear communication between all the multidisciplinary team as they came into contact with the people involved. Working within a team and recognising and reacting appropriately to the grieving process.

How has this incident affected your practice?
The incident has demonstrated to me the difference between dealing with the dying child and the adult and highlighted the areas where skills are transferable in each situation.

Analysing Example I

For this critical incident a thinking strategy was applied in the analysis of the experience. The analysis was on the observation of another professional's practice. The nurse was able to draw on learning from the situation and then analyse the practice to identify how she would deal with a similar situation in her own practice. The incident allowed the nurse to reflect on the scientific knowledge that she had been taught in the classroom, i.e. theory relating to care of the dying patient and the importance of good communication skills; caring in an holistic approach; and support for the relatives as they go through the grieving process before and following the death of the child. The incident included other issues that were relevant to this situation: for example, the importance of team work within the clinical environment and the role of the multidisciplinary team in the care of the dying child. Following Tripp's (1993) analysis of critical incidents, certain thinking strategies had been used in this situation as the incident allowed the observer to reflect on the incident and apply scientific knowledge to practice, identifying gaps in that knowledge that may require further study or research. In this case, gaps might have included theory relating to the grieving process and/or models of communication and counselling. This 'thinking strategies' approach reminds us to consider alternative views and perhaps what did not actually happen. In this situation, what Tripp refers to as the 'non-events' may also prove valuable to the nurse reflecting on this situation. For example, what if this had not gone to plan or some situation had arisen in the comforting of these parents that made the incident a negative process? The nurse might then have wanted to reflect on the situation should the named nurse not have been present, or if she was dealing with a child that she had not had the opportunity to gain a relationship with.

Critical incident analysis used for continuing professional development

Many professional bodies require the practitioner to identify areas and ways of maintaining and continuing their professional development and their personal development plan for the KSF. This can be obtained through learning during practice, and documented carefully in the ways we are suggesting. It is this practice knowledge that, if recorded and interrogated, can be used for the professional profile/plan.

Example 2: Critical incident analysis

Description of incident
On being in charge of the ward as a newly qualified nurse the consultant identified that he and the relatives did not want a patient to be informed of his diagnosis and prognosis. This was a cancer that meant he had a very poor prognosis. On talking with the patient, with whom I had a good relationship, he asked me if he had cancer, as he wanted to sort things out for himself. I did not inform him and he died one week later, never being formally told what was wrong. From the time of this conversation our relationship disintegrated, as he knew I was withholding information.

By whom was it handled?
The ward round where this information was given was handled by myself, and instructions were passed on to other shifts.

What learning occurred?
In this situation I felt that my trust was being questioned as conflict occurred between what I had been told by the consultant and relatives and what the patient was asking. For myself I learned that although they were attempting to protect the patient, he needed to sort himself out and therefore there was a problem with communication between all those involved in his care.

What were the outcomes of this incident?
To listen to all the patient's requests and not to compromise trust and destroy relationships that have been built up. To discuss these issues with all the team and the relatives if the patient is asking for more information, as he may have appreciated the truth and prepared himself for a more peaceful death, dealing with his affairs and being able to say goodbye.

How has this incident affected your practice?
To be more assertive with medical staff and to work as a team, keeping them informed of the patient's wishes. To act as a patient's advocate in the giving of information and maintaining their trust.

Analysing Example 2

Dilemma identification and analysis is where a conflict between personal values and beliefs and hospital values and beliefs arises. Analysis of these incidents can identify, for the individual, their own value system, areas of poor or inappropriate practice, and situations where communication is problematic or where patient advocacy may be a potential problem between professionals. The first process here is to identify that a dilemma and conflict of beliefs and/or values is occurring. Then one needs to analyse how to act in the best interests of clients, colleagues or peers, supported by appropriate professional and/or legislative procedures. In accordence with the Nurses, Midwives and Health Visitors Code of Professional Conduct (2002), the practitioner must act in the best interests of the individual and observe their own limitations, working collaboratively with other members of the multidisciplinary team. Often some practices can cause personal conflict between what Carper (1978) referred to as our ethical knowledge (see Chapter 1) and the values that the institution holds. For example, an individual's institution may promote a non-smoking policy. The individual, however, may believe that smoking should be permitted for the patients. The conflict caused may result in the nurse experiencing some frustration, but it is not harmful to colleagues or patients and therefore the individual must suppress their behaviour and conform to the policy of the institution. Example 2 identifies a dilemma for a newly qualified practitioner in that he is placed in a situation where one health care professional disagrees with his beliefs and he is left to administer the conflicting care prescribed. The inexperience of the newly qualified practitioner may later be used in his professional profile to identify where he has developed professionally and become more assertive. He may be able to demonstrate an increased ability to justify his actions as he becomes more experienced in dealing with other professionals and those in more senior positions than himself. The situation could equally be used at a job interview to identify how he has learned through practice and how a change in his practice has occurred through the situation.

Critical incident analysis for accreditation of prior experiential learning

For accreditation of prior experiential learning (APEL), individual practitioners are attempting to identify where learning has occurred through their clinical practice and how they can then apply their underlying theories to their practice, thus identifying levels of *competence*. In many situations the APEL procedure may require more analysis of the incident to identify reflection and learning in relation to developing and moving their practice forward. For the APEL process individuals may be asked to present their incidents in the form of an essay. For the following example the same format as for the job interview andprofessional requirements has been used.

Example 3: Critical incident analysis

Description of incident
Over a period of three months the Home was told that we should introduce a model of nursing into our practice. As the charge nurse I put this to the team and it was decided to discuss this and devise a model of nursing that was appropriate to the care we gave. To implement and evaluate this change in practice actually took the team one year.

By whom was it handled?
Myself in conjunction with all the members of the Home staff. Management and senior staff were consulted during and after our meetings to approve what was being discussed and to comment on the changes that were being implemented.

What learning occurred?
This proved to be a large area of learning for me as an individual, as primarily I had to review all the models available in practice. This involved external visits to other homes to see how they were using them. How to develop a model was then undertaken and the change process was used to incorporate the change successfully'

What were the outcomes of this incident?
As an individual I learned about the development of nursing models, how to lead a group of practitioners through a process of change and the problems that arise within a group of people, with all the negotiation that has to occur between the practitioners and the management structures. It also identified the time it actually took to implement new procedures and the legal implications of such a process.

How has this incident affected your practice?
It has identified the theory and practice of nursing, also gaining knowledge concerned with changing practice. The importance of gaining all the team's support when attempting to make such a major change in practice and the importance of evaluating of that change.

Analysing Example 3

In this situation the 'Why?' question can be applied to analyse the situation. As discussed in Chapter 5, the question 'Why?' is asked to analyse the underlying values that are held by that practitioner. The analysis of this experience identifies how the individual's practice has developed or may have potentially developed inappropriately. Example 3 could be used as an example of where learning has occurred as the practitioner attempts to identify improvements in an area of practice. To deepen the analysis the Why? challenge could be applied to find out why the change was necessary? Other why-type questions that penetrate deep into this incident might be, 'Why did it take a year?'; 'Why were the senior managers consulted?'; 'Why were visits to other homes necessary?'; and so on.

This chapter has provided several examples of incidents that can be analysed using a variety of methods. The incident should be written in such a way to protect individuals and preserve their anonymity. The ethical issues identified in the earlier chapter with regard to journal writing are also pertinent to the writing and sharing of analyses of critical incidents.

References

Carper, B. (1978) Fundamental patterns of knowing. *Advances in Nursing Science*, **1**, 13–23.

Department of Health (2004)*The NHS Knowledge and Skills Framework (NHS KSF) and the Development Review Process*. Department of Health, London.

Tripp, D. (1993)*Critical Incidents in Teaching: Developing Critical Judgement*. Routledge, London.

Nursing and Midwifery Council (2002) *Professional Code of Conduct*. UKCC, London.

PART 3

Outcomes

CHAPTER 7

Implications for practice

The professional journal and the analysis of critical incidents are two ways to facilitate learning. If undertaken systematically and deliberatively they have the potential to impact on practice in three broad ways. We have grouped these under the following headings:

- **Technical**: how the two processes help the health care professional to achieve something concrete and instrumental. In this sense they can be seen as means to clearly specified ends. Examples of this are fulfilling the PREP and KSF requirements, undertaking clinical supervision effectively, addressing the issue of becoming more accountable as stipulated in the Code of Professional Conduct, and preparing an APEL claim.
- **Practical**: how the two processes facilitate, nourish and sustain our ability to make wise, competent and ethical decisions and to act compassionately and truly given the clinical context. Examples of this are clarifying the nature of our professional values, engaging in meaningful dialogues and deepening our understanding of the links between practice and theory.
- **Emancipatory**: how the two learning processes help us to question the status quo, the taken-for-grantedness of our clinical worlds and the historical, social and political forces that serve to liberate and constrain our work. Examples of this are the ways in which the professional journal and the analysis of critical incidents generate nursing knowledge and can help to develop the critically reflective practitioner.

Technical

1: Post-Registration, Education and Practice requirements (PREP) and Personal Development Plans

PREP came into being in April 1995 and the Personal Development Plan, through KSF, in 2004. The PREP requirements affect every registered Nurse, Midwife and Health Visitor (Nursing and Midwifery Council, 2004), and Personal Development Plans apply across the whole of the NHS for all staff with the exception of doctors, dentists and some senior and board level staff who have other arrangements for their development (Department of Health, 2004). The PREP document states that all practitioners must demonstrate their continuing development and how this relates to their clinical competence. This should then be recorded in a personal professional profile (Nursing and Midwifery Council, 2004) . Many practitioners may argue that they have always developed their skills and competence. The difference is that since 1995, following the introduction of PREP (United Kingdom Central Council, 1990), everyone needed to *demonstrate* professional development through the profile. The journal and analysis of critical incidents are valuable sources of evidence of professional development for the individual. Both represent learning accomplishments, future needs and wants. There is no reason why this evidence should not be incorporated into the 'personal professional profile'.

2: Undertaking clinical supervision

In the UK government's policy statement *Vision for the Future* (Department of Health, 1993), all health care professionals were being urged to enhance their practice, become competent in self-assessment and develop analytical and reflective skills. The document links this clearly to clinical supervision (Department of Health, 1993, p. 15):

> It (clinical supervision) is central to the process of learning and to the expansion of the scope of practice and should be seen as a means of encouraging self-assessment, analytical and reflective skills.

Keeping a professional journal is predicated upon the fact that the practitioner is reflective. Critical incidents become a source of learning and lead to improved clinical action because they require an analysis of practice. Both processes, if done rigorously and systematically over time, can produce reasoned and wise practical knowledge. The practitioner and clinical supervisor can interrogate this knowledge and share insights and experiences with the intention of improving the quality of care given.

3: Addressing the Code of Professional Conduct

The nurse, midwife and health visitor's Code of Professional Conduct (Nursing and Midwifery Council, 2002) states that each practitioner is '*accountable*' for their own practice, that they must update their practice, acknowledge their personal limitations and, at all times, be able to justify what they do. This is a big agenda. Justifying practice is about professional accountability. If the professional journal and analysis of critical incidents become true 'companions' for all health carers, then the evidence they contain can be used to articulate the different ways in which practice can be justified. Through both processes strengths are identified, limitations appreciated and action plans formulated.

4: Preparing an APEL claim

For many, the introduction of the credit accumulation and transfer system (CATS), has added much needed flexibility to learning. At the heart of this system is the module, which carries with it a CATS rating, usually in the form of 'points' and at given 'level'. Points are accumulated upon the successful completion of modules. The points build up towards the specified award. Among other things, modularity, ratings and CATS have opened up the issue of practitioners being accredited: that is, being given credit for successful formal study undertaken before entry to the current course (APL – the accreditation of prior learning) and for prior experiential learning (APEL). Evidence for the APEL has to be provided by the applicant to the course. The professional journal and the analysis of critical incidents are an excellent source for such evidence of learning from experience.

Practical

1: *Clarifying the nature of our professional values*

Central to any professional improvement effort is an understanding of the relevance and potency of professional values. Health care is value-based work (Ghaye *et al.* 1996a, p. 19):

> We believe that a fundamental type of knowledge that health care professionals need is what we shall call their 'values-based knowledge'. The constituents of this knowledge are the caregiver's professional values, which give a shape, form and purpose to what they do in their clinical areas. This knowledge is not just linked to practice, but also tied inextricably to – and derived from – that practice. Values-based knowledge informs and constantly transforms practice. The problem is that often we do not know the values we have.

Knowledge for responsible and competent clinical action is knowledge where value positions, values in action, and contradictions between what we say and do are explicit and justified. The processes of journal writing and critical incident analysis can help to bring out into the open the values that make us the kind of health care professionals we are.

2: *Engaging in meaningful dialogues*

Dialogues of this kind sustain and nourish organisational cultures for improvement. Dialogues can be with self and/or others. They can raise individual and organisational consciousness. Journal writing and the analysis of critical incidents, as we have depicted them, are personally meaningful dialogues which contain reference to individuals, tasks and a clinical context. The dialogues can be those of:

- **Possibility**: if they reflect not only what was thought and done, but what might have been. In other words that 'which is not yet'.
- **Hope**: if they describe, explain and justify how the health care professional tries to bring about relevant, appropriate and ethically grounded improvements in their practice and workplace.
- **Confrontation**: if they interrogate practice and avoid celebrating it uncritically.

- **Liberation**: as they should contain a discourse about health care couched in a language, and in a form, that is personally created and owned by the writer and not imposed upon them.

3: Deepening our understanding of the links between practice and theory (see Ghaye et al., 1996b)

In writing this book we have alluded to the fact that we do not believe that it is useful to approach the notions of practice and theory as if they were separate entities which have to be fitted together somehow. We also believe that it is simplistic to think that in fitting things together some new and wonderful insights and actions will arise, in an almost magical way! Journal entries and critical incidents point up two conceptions of 'practical theory'. The first is that they represent 'theory-as-content'. That is, they both contain content which can be seen as a body of health care knowledge which is known by oneself, and might usefully be known by others. The second is that they represent 'theory-as-process'. By this we mean that it is through the writing of a professional journal and the analysis of critical incidents that we engage in the process of 'theorising' about our clinical practice. This process reflects an interactive view of practice and theory where ideas guide our thinking and actions and where clinical practice informs and transforms ideas (Cox *et al.*, 1991, p. 378):

> Reconstruction of nursing practice and the practice worlds of nurses may occur through this process

Emancipatory

What should be clear at this stage is that the professional journal and critical incidents symbolise much more than ways to solve practical problems. They are not merely 'tools' or 'techniques'. This is a truncated definition and misrepresents their full nature and power. We are arguing that they can act as a dynamic source of ideas and actions which have the potential to raise very fundamental questions about the nature of our professionality, how this is understood, and how it interacts with practice and generates practical workplace change.

In a very important sense they represent an attempt to discover, understand and then perhaps improve existing patterns and order. This is a vital part of the practitioner's meaning-making process. Accounts of practice often draw upon descriptors such as 'turbulent' and 'chaotic'. Journal writing and critical incident analysis are a commitment to come to know, more deeply and richly, the pattern and order in our clinical work, for we live in a universe of patterns (Stewart, 1995, pp. 1–3):

> Every night the stars move in circles across the sky. The seasons cycle at yearly intervals. No two snowflakes are ever exactly the same, but they all have a sixfold symmetry. Tigers and zebras are covered in patterns of stripes, leopards and hyenas are covered in patterns of spots. Intricate trains of waves march across the oceans; very similar trains of sand dunes march across the desert. Coloured arcs of light adorn the sky in the form of rainbows, and a bright circular halo sometimes surrounds the moon on winter nights.... Patterns possess utility as well as beauty. Once we have learned to recognise a background pattern, exceptions suddenly stand out. The desert stands still but the lion moves.

Both the professional journal and pro formas for the analysis of critical incidents may, at this moment, be empty and just waiting for you to make a start. We hope that this book helps you to think through the nature of your commitment to these two learning processes.

> I have a dream. I am surrounded by – nothing. Not empty space, for there is no space to be empty. Not blackness, for there is nothing to be black. Simply an absence, waiting to become a presence. (Stewart, 1995, p. vii)

References

Cox, H., Hickson, P. and Taylor, B. (1991) Exploring reflection: knowing and constructing practice. In *Towards a Discipline of Nursing* (ed. G. Gray and R. Pratt). Churchill Livingstone, Melbourne.

Department of Health (1993) *Vision for the Future*. HMSO, London.

Department of Health (2004) *The NHS Knowledge and Skills Framework (NHS KSF) and the Development Review Process*. Department of Health, London.

Ghaye, T. *et al.* (1996a) *Professional Values: Being a Professional*. Formword, Newcastle-upon-Tyne.

Ghaye, T. *et al.* (1996b) *Theory–Practice Relationships: Reconstructing Practice*. Formword, Newcastle-upon-Tyne.

Nursing and Midwifery Council (2002) *Professional Code of Conduct*. UKCC, London.

Nursing and Midwifery Council (2004) *The PREP Handbook*. Nursing and Midwifery Council, London.

Stewart, I. (1995) *Nature's Numbers: Discovering Order and Pattern in the Universe*. Weidenfeld & Nicolson, London.

United Kingdom Central Council (1990) *The Report of Post-Registration Education and Practice Project*. UKCC, London.

Conclusion

The topography of health care is a challenging one to understand and navigate our way through. It is a value-laden landscape comprised of different knowledges, power structures and political orientations. It is a dynamic landscape where human relations, opportunities for personal growth and the culture of clinical environments constantly change. It is also a perceptual landscape where health care professionals, clients and their families have differing views and experiences of 'real', 'ideal' and 'expected' quality care. Reflective practice is not only a way of 'reading the map' but also provides opportunities to 'transform the map' and to reconfigure it.

This book has had four principal elements to it. First there has been a *descriptive* element associated with questions like, 'What is reflective practice?' and 'What are learning journals and critical incidents?'. Secondly, there has been a *dialogic* element. For example, we have said that keeping a learning journal, among other things, gives us the chance to have reflective conversations with self, others and the clinical environment. Critical incident analysis was portrayed as a catalyst for meaningful dialogue between peers, managers, clinical supervisors and so on. Thirdly, the book has contained a *critical* element. By this we mean that learning through journal writing and the analysis of critical incidents gives us a greater awareness of self as human agent and the politico-economic and socio-historical influences which serve to regulate practice. It is through these two processes that we can question the taken-for-grantedness of our clinical worlds. The process is a potentially destabilising one. This leads us on to the fourth and final element, which is an *action-oriented* one. Just to question things daily does not mean that anything will improve. Action is required. One outcome of reflection is that it should have a consequence. Through reflection-on-action we should come to know the wise, competent and ethical thing to do and have the courage and skills to do and defend it. Through these two learning processes, insights, appreciations and commitments to act are enriched and consolidated. The learning which accrues can affirm or challenge why we continue to practice in the way we do.

Throughout the book we have drawn attention to the importance of the 'local', to clinical action in a local context. We have focused on the micro-level, where health care professionals observe, experience and influence (to a greater or lesser extent!) different forms of domination, resistance, facilitation and commitments to quality care delivery. The content of learning journals and the nature of critical incidents often identifies when and how care-giving situations and health care systems are either sustained or break down. Reflection-on-action, through these two processes of learning, provides the possibility of generating and implementing strategies for improvement that might actually work.

But we cannot create and enter a better world if we cannot envision and articulate it. The use of learning journals and critical incidents can help us do just this. Both are media through which health care professionals create accounts (or 'texts') of what they claim they know and what they want or are able to do with this knowledge of practice-in-context. Each text is often part of a 'tangle-of-texts' (Sumara and Luce-Kapler, 1993), which convey a sense of the tensions, dilemmas and contradictions between the health carer as a human agent, on the one hand, and organisational structures on the other.

Reflection-on-action, in the ways we have set out in this book, have the potential to transform our practice and the clinical context in which it takes place. 'All in a day's work' becomes much, much more than habitual, routine and taken-for-granted practice. Learning journals and critical incidents are gateways to a deeper, inner reflection upon ourselves and others, how we wish to be in the world and how we might improve it. In this sense this book aligns itself with a general view of reflective practice that is a continuing struggle both to:

- empower the individual through personal and socio-political conscious raising
- empower groups through collective action to build contexts for care that are more just, democratic, compassionate and dignified.

Reference

Sumara, D. and Luce-Kapler, R. (1993) Action research as a writerly text: locating co-labouring in collaboration. *Educational Action Research*, **1**, 387–95.

Index